Contents

Incidence and Prevalence of Sex Crimes • Legal
Concerns • The Offender's Sexual Behavior •
Danger to the Community • Without Victim
Consent • Offense Context • Conviction • Clini-
cal Profiles • Heterogeneity • Pedophiles • Sexual
Assault Offenders • Intellectually Disabled Sex •
Offenders • Female Sex Offenders • Are Sex Of-
fenders Mentally Ill? • Multiple Paraphilias •
Treatment or Punishment? • Can Sex Offenders
Change?

Biological Influences • Childhood Experiences •
Parents • Discipline • Loneliness • Masturbatory
Fantasies • Sociocultural Context • Availability of
Pornography • Immediate Circumstances • Sum-
mary

Overcoming Skepticism • What Is Good Sex Offender Treatment? • Goals of Treatment • Expect
Denial • Assessment • Psychophysiological Testing • Molester Plethysmograph Profile • Plethysmograph Profile • Vaginal Probe • Clinical
Polygraph • The Interview • Principles for Interviewing Sex Offenders • Collateral Information •
Psychological Tests

Behavioral Treatment • Boredom Tapes • Covert
Sensitization • Aversive Conditioning • Orgasmic
Reconditioning • Cognitive Restructuring • Seven

Mistaken Beliefs of Sex Offenders • Changing
Cognitions • Sex Offender Groups • Medication •
Re-education and Resocialization • Gender Role
Behavior • Sexuality • Personal Victimization and
Trauma • Empathy • Assertiveness Training and
Resocialization Skills • Family Skills • Chemical
Use and Abuse Groups • Relapse Prevention •
Treating Intellectually-Disabled Sex Offenders •
Disabled and Nondisabled Sex Offenders • Cop-
ing and Learning Skills • Treatment Methods •
Treating Female Sex Offenders • Summary

Treatment • Restitution Requirements • Community Service Requirements • Court Reviews • Departmental Reviews • Rules of Supervision • Initial Interview of the Sex Offender • No-contact and Residency Rules • Other Special Provisions • Employment Status • Home Visits • Travel Permits • Notification of Law Enforcement • Intrastate and Interstate Transfer and Direct Assignment Cases • Violations and Revocation Issues • New Allegations of Sexual Offenses • Revocation Procedures • Preparole Plans • Discharge • Victims of Sex Offenses • The Effects of Sexual Victimization • Child Victims • Sexual Abuse in the Family • Adult Victims of Sex Crimes • Conclusion

Illustrations

Figures

Tables

Foreword

Over the past several decades we have observed major changes in this country in the way the criminal justice system responds to sex crimes. The plight of the victims has been given greater attention, and victim/witness units have been developed to help victims with court testimony, protection, and restitution. Court orders and supervision rules now often restrict the offender's contact with past or potential victims. Increasingly, incest perpetrators, rather than the child victims, are removed from their homes. Many agencies — law enforcement, district attorneys, child protective services, community supervision and corrections, and parole — now provide specialized programming for handling sexual assault cases.

Judges have adjusted sentencing practices to include probation coupled with jail time as a condition. Psychological evaluation and therapy are also often included as conditions of probation.

With these changes there has been an increased in the numbers and types of sex offenders committed to probation and released on parole. For supervising officers this has meant learning new skills.

This book was written to offer supervising officers, child protective service workers, human service workers, counselors, judges, and district attorneys with a more systematic statement about the supervision and treatment of sex offenders. The author hopes that those who already have a solid foundation in this area will find major issues pulled together in one convenient place. For practitioners new to this topic, this book can hopefully offer practical help and guidance.

The reader should keep in mind that this field of inquiry is subject to rapid change as new developments and approaches are developed. Consequently, this book is not meant to be the last word or the complete answer to every question about supervising this clientele. As with any type of client, there are no hard and fast rules which can be applied in every case. Here, as always, common sense is probably the most important principle.

This book, originally designed to assist public servants in the State of Texas who handle sex offenders, had as its model an earlier effort by correctional employees in the Wisconsin Division of Corrections. Representatives from the Bureaus of Community Corrections and Clinical Services in that state led by James Wake produced a landmark work in 1989 entitled *Sex Offender Supervision Handbook*. Their efforts provided the starting point for this book, and the author appreciates their cooperation in giving us permission to borrow from their work. The chapters on the presentence investigation and supervision reflect much of the legwork done by the Wisconsin group.

Acknowledgments

A debt of gratitude is owed to the members of the Advisory Board who reviewed the original proposal and edited the first draft of the manuscript. Their excellent suggestions markedly improved the product and, hopefully, have increased its usefulness to practitioners.

This project would not have been possible without the encouragement of Dean Charles Friel, who first proposed the project and provided invaluable support. He also made funds available to support the development of this book.

I also appreciate the encouragement and assistance given to me by my wife, Melanie. She not only reviewed and edited early drafts of this book, but was patient with my preoccupation in writing it. She, along with my children, have provided the loving support which helped me in completing this project.

A volume published by the National Institute of Corrections entitled *Treatment Skills for Professionals Working with Sex Offenders* also contributed to the completion of this effort. Several books published by the Safer Society were particularly helpful in addressing the intellectually disabled sex offender and the female sex offender. A workshop sponsored by the American Probation and Parole Association in Austin, Texas and presented by William Pithers from the Vermont Treatment Program for Sexual Aggressives on Relapse Prevention also contributed to completing the chapter on treatment.

1

Sex Offender Profiles

Over the past three decades our society has become increasingly aware of how frequently acts of sexual aggression occur. At first, most of the concern was on the severe consequences suffered by victims, while sex offenders were viewed as simply moral and social degenerates who deserved long periods of imprisonment or even death. The criminal justice system, during this period, recognized three alternatives for itself in dealing with sex offenders. These included punishing sex offenders by sentencing them to a specified number of years in correctional facilities • placing offenders in state mental health institutions for treatment for unspecified periods, and • providing court-ordered probation, sometimes coupled with various forms of treatment. For various reasons, it has been the punitive alternative that is commonly employed by the criminal justice system for dealing with sex offenders. Yet it has become increasingly clear that a strictly punitive approach to managing sex offenders is simply incapable of preventing reoffenses — that is, sex offenders are locked up, let out, and then commit more sex offenses. Furthermore, responding to sex offenders with punishment alone is unreasonably expensive, and it is usually inconsistently applied.

Also, it is unrealistic to expect the problem of sexual victimization to be resolved by limiting attention to convicted sex offenders. Research on victimization rates and perpetrator offense patterns show that only a small percentage of offenders are ever apprehended and, even those who are, rarely serve long prison terms or receive treatment. It can be argued that imprisonment as commonly practiced is far from being a deterrent to reoffending. Rather, it only increases an offender's tendency and ability to commit sexual assaults.

A growing number of authorities now agree that breaking the chain of sexual aggression requires not only legal sanctions and effective treatment with convicted offenders but with prevention activities as well.

Incidence and Prevalence of Sex Crimes

According to one U.S. Department of Justice report, *Sex Offenses and Offenders* (Greenfield 1997), in 1995 there were nearly 355,000 reported rapes and other sexual assaults to victims 12 years of age or older. Other studies suggest an even larger number of victims. The *Sourcebook of Criminal Statistics* (1996), reported 316,140 victims of rape or attempted rape, and another 116,570 victims of other forms of sexual assault among persons 12 years of age or older. Add to the these figures the number of children who are victims of sexual crimes in a year and the magnitude of the trauma caused by sex offenders seems overwhelming.

What is worse is that these figures for reported victimizations, do not, in any sense, provide a true estimate of the magnitude of sexual assault. A variety of studies clearly document something that law enforcement officers and social workers experience nearly every day — that only a small proportion of victims of sexual crime report their victimization to authorities. The actual number of sex crimes may be as much as 20 times greater than the numbers reported.

Reasonable lifetime estimates of the likelihood of becoming a sexual assault victim are 50 percent for women and 15 percent for men (Kilpatrick et al. 1987). A study (Able et al. 1987) of sex offenders in outpatient treatment revealed that offenders commit an average of 2.02 different types of illegal sexual acts. The number of acts committed and victims assaulted, however, varied widely by type of offense. The typical rapist commits an average of 7.2 sexual assaults against seven victims, and child molesters offending against male victims outside the family commit an average of 281.7 assaults against 150.2 victims. This study of 561 sex offenders who came into treatment voluntarily revealed that these offenders committed an average of 520 offenses per person and that the number of victims totaled 195,407! The average age of the offenders was 31.5. If the age of onset is adolescence for a majority of offenders, then these offenders had been committing sexually deviant acts for more than a decade.

It is helpful to break down the offenses by type to see how the numbers of acts and victims vary. Incest offenders commit a high number of acts against a low number of victims compared to offenders who molest children outside the home. This finding simply underscores the long-term periods of time over which incest often occurs and the limits of family size. Nonetheless, the figures indicate that a sizable proportion of offenders molested more than one child in the family.

Those who molested girls outside the family engaged in fewer sexual acts than did incest offenders. However, men who molested boys outside the family had a dramatically higher number of offenses than male-oriented incest offenders. This is not to suggest that offenders who target children outside the home are a different group of offenders who molest more children, because, as will be pointed out later, incest offenders also occasionally molest outside the home. The evidence does suggest that sex offenders who target male children outside the family have more victims, are more repetitive, and begin their offending careers at earlier ages. Clinical reports suggest they are more difficult to treat than other offenders and have higher recidivism rates (Salter 1989).

Interestingly, the types of sexual behaviors likely to have the highest rates of occurrence are exhibitionism, voyeurism, and the practice of getting sexual stimulation by rubbing against another person (i.e., frottage) as opposed to such acts as fondling, intercourse, and oral sex.

Sex Offenders (according to the law)

- are persons,
- engage in criminal sexual behavior,
- engage in sexual behavior without the consent of the victim,
- present a danger to the community, and
- have been convicted of a crime.

It is conservatively estimated that one in 60 sexual crimes actually leads to arrest. Together all of the reported findings indicate that adult male sexual aggression and subsequent sexual victimization are serious social problems that affect a large portion of the population.

Legal Concerns

When the probation or parole officer reads the criminal complaint, police reports, and other information, it is important to remember that the sex offender is a person. All kinds of people commit sex crimes. Such behavior is not unique to any one social, economic, or racial group. People who commit sex crimes may have traditional values and have not necessarily had previous involvement with the legal system. He or she may or may not be mentally ill. In some instances, the person may be a prominent member of the community.

The officer must be able to get beyond his or her discomfort about discussing the intimate details of a client's sexual desires and conduct, and to overcome personal distaste for the bizarre and predatory quality of most sex offender behavior if he or she is to recognize the offender's primary quality of being a person. In other words, the officer must learn to separate the offender from the offending behavior.

It is important to be able to classify sex offenders according to their preferences and characteristic behaviors but the resulting labels should not blur the distinction between the person and the behavior. If the offender is not seen as a person, it will be difficult to establish a basis for the important discussions necessary for providing good supervision. Important to an officer's effectiveness in supervision is the ability to discuss with the offender issues such as intimacy, difficulties with dangerous sexual urges and fantasies, victim empathy, and human relationships in the offender's life.

The Offender's Sexual Behavior

In order to understand a sex offender, the officer needs to know the facts surrounding the offenses. Did physical sexual behavior occur or was it an attempt? Was the behavior planned or was it impulsive? Was the victim penetrated? Was penetration vaginal, anal, oral? Were foreign objects used and was the victim physically harmed in other ways? Was the behavior in question performed only on the victim or on the offender as well? Was a weapon involved? Were threats made against the victim? Answers to these questions provide the basis for a clearer understanding of the offense, the victim, and often the case management. (See Table 1.1 illustrating a variety of crimes.)

Officers need to be aware that they cannot count on the accuracy of the offender's versions of the crime. Statements about

Table 1.1 Sex Crimes in Texas*

Sexual Assault

A person:

- intentionally or knowingly
- without the consent of the victim or with a person less than 17 years of age, through the use of threat of force or violence, or when the victim is unconscious or physically unable to resist, or the victim is drugged;
- engages in penetration of the mouth, vagina, or anus of another person (not his or her spouse) by any means; or
- engages in penetration of the mouth, vagina, or anus of the actor by the sexual organ of another person (not his or her spouse)

Aggravated Sexual Assault

A person:

- engages in sexual assault, and
- threatens or causes serious bodily injury to the victim, or
- threatens or attempts to cause the death of the victim, or
- places the victim in fear that death, serious bodily injury, or kidnapping will be inflicted on anyone.

Indecent Exposure

A person exposes his anus or any part of his genitals with the intent to arouse or gratify the sexual desire of any person, and is reckless about whether another person is present who will be offended or alarmed by his act.

Indecency with a Child

A person engages in sexual contact with a child under 17 years of age who is not his spouse, or exposes his anus or any part of his genitals, knowing the child is present, with the intent to arouse or gratify the sexual desire of any person.

Prohibited Sexual Conduct

A person engages in sexual intercourse or contact between the genitals of one person and the mouth or anus of another with a person he knows to be

- his ancestor or descendant by blood or adoption
- his stepchild or stepparent (if that person is still married to a relative)
- an aunt or uncle (either whole or half)
- a brother or sister (either whole or half or by adoption)
- a niece or nephew (either whole or half or by adoption)

Solicitation of a Child

A person entices, persuades, or invites a child less than 14 years of age to enter a vehicle, building, structure, or enclosed area with the intent to engage in or propose to engage in sexual intercourse, contact between the genitals of one person and the mouth or anus of another, sexual contact with, or exposure of his anus or any part of his genitals to the child.

Sexual Performance by a Child

A person employs, authorizes, or induces a child younger than 17 years of age to engage in a sexual conduct or a sexual performance. A parent or legal guardian or custodian of a child commits an offense if he consents to the participation by the child in a sexual performance.

---

*Please note that state laws vary. The reader should be familiar with the laws in his or her state.

guilt or the details of what happened most often are inaccurate or incomplete. More reliable sources of information may be victim statements to police or other law enforcement information. Reliance on offender reports concerning details of the criminal behavior are almost always inaccurate (Abel 1985). Consequently, victim statements to police or other law enforcement reports are critical to obtaining accurate information about the offender's behavior.

Danger to the Community

Assessing how dangerous an offender is to the community should begin with the recognition that all sexually assaultive behaviors pose a threat. Of course, the most dramatic examples are assaultive acts on strangers: a rape committed in the course of a burglary or robbery • a series of rapes following a pattern of stalking victims • child molestation by pedophiles. The worst sex offenses may be accompanied by abduction, severe bodily mutilation, or even death.

Other illegal but equally predatory sexual behaviors may involve victims known to the offender: intrafamilial child sexual abuse • date or spouse rape • sexual victimization of persons with reduced capacity for consent (e.g., mentally or physically handicapped persons).

Examples of criminal but less dramatic sexual behaviors include producing some forms of pornography, indecent exposure, sexual behavior with animals, voyeurism, and prostitution.

Other gauges of the level of danger an offender represents to the community include past offender behaviors and how much responsibility he or she takes for these behaviors.

Without Victim Consent

In many respects, all criminal sexual behavior involves the nonconsent of the victim (with perhaps the exception of prostitution), but the level of nonconsent may vary from one crime to the other. The victim with reduced capacity to give consent is also harmed by sexual assault in much the same way as the non-consenting victim of rape. Some of the conditions that reduce a person's capacity to give consent include age (children), physical condition (drugged), mental ability (developmentally disabled), or power abuse (therapists' patients). The issue of victim nonconsent is important for the officer to understand because many sex offenders will argue that the victim "wanted it" or "came on" to them. To many of these individuals this perception then justifies their actions.

Offense Context

Most sex crimes don't just happen. Instead, they are often part of a long-standing pattern of antisocial behavior, or they are driven by a value system that justifies predatory acts. Determining whether the criminal behavior in question was an isolated act or part of a larger context is important in deciding how to effectively supervise the offender. Is the offender developmentally disabled and incapable of grasping society's values concerning sexual behavior? Does he or she have mental health issues at the source of criminal sexual behavior? Is the choice of sexual object induced by stress or does it represent the offender's usual sexual orientation?

Conviction

The most definitive description of the sex offender comes from the statutes. The court order convicting the offender reduces behavior to a statute number, a one phrase crime designation, and a criminal complaint. Useful discussion about the sex offender can only occur after the officer is familiar with the sections of the penal code which pertain to sex crimes. The officer should be knowledgeable about the degrees of severity spelled out in the laws for the various sex offenses. Each degree of sexual assault is based on aspects of the offense, such as age of the victim, level of violence associated with the act, or mental ability of the victim.

Clinical Profiles

Most of us react negatively to the label "sex offender." It conjures up images of "sex fiends" or of the largely mythical "dirty old man." Misconceptions about sex offenders are common among professionals as well as lay persons. What Groth asserted in 1978 is still true:

> The child sex offender [is imagined], "to be a stranger, an old man, insane or retarded, alcohol or drug addicted, sexually frustrated and impotent or sexually jaded, and looking for new "kicks." . . . He is sometimes regarded as a brutal sex fiend or a shy, passive, sexually inexperienced person. He is oversexed or he is undersexed, . . . the product of a sexually permissive and immoral society . . . [that encourages] him through the availability of pornography, prostitution, drugs, alcohol, and sex outside of marriage" (Groth 1978).

There are cases that tend to support each of these notions, but they are the exception rather than the rule. These popular beliefs serve to perpetuate the myth of the child molester or rapist as different and unlike the ordinary person as possible. The appeal of this approach is that it takes a very complex behavior with multiple causes and reduces it to a stereotype with a few simple causes. The resulting stereotypes and overgeneralizations are easier to understand and accept than the reality. However, this simplistic reduction is actually a barrier to helping sex offenders overcome their problems.

Heterogeneity

The population that is responsible for the commission of sex offenses is extremely heterogeneous. There is no single profile that describes sex offenders. Offenders with widely varying criminal histories, who differ in age, background, personality, psychiatric diagnosis, race, and religion, all get grouped together because they have engaged in illegal sexual activity. Their offenses too have also varied markedly with respect to location and time, the sex and age of the victim, the degree of planning, and the amount of violence. Despite this diversity sex offenders are often viewed as a homogeneous class of offenders.

In actuality, the sex offender may be a close relative, friend, or acquaintance rather than a stranger; an older person or an adolescent; wealthy or poor; White or Black; gay or straight; religious or nonreligious; a professional, white- or blue-collar, or unemployed worker; and a person with an extensive criminal record or one with no recorded offense history. Although they are usually males, females also commit sex offenses.

Even with the complexities in trying to develop comprehensive classification schemes, several typologies have been offered. For example, Groth's (1978, 1979) classifications of **power, anger,** and **sadistic rapists,** and **fixated** and **regressed pedophiles** are used by many treatment specialists. (See Tables 1.2, 1.3, and 1.4.)

Pedophiles

Groth's identification of the fixated/regressed dimension in classifying child molesters has gained wide acceptance in the literature. Most pedophile typologies at least include this dimension, and it is a good idea to be familiar with his scheme.

Dietz's (1983) — also still widely used — typology of child molesters is formulated around Groth's two broad categories — **situational** (regressed) versus **preferential** (fixated) offenders — but expands them to include subtypes (see Table 1.3). The situational offenders category is subdivided to include the regressed, morally indiscriminate, sexually indiscriminate and inadequate offenders. The preferential offenders category includes the seductive, introverted and sadistic offenders. This classification scheme

Table 1.2
Typology of Pedophilia

Fixated	Regressed
1. Primary sexual orientation is to children	1. Primary sexual orientation is to agemates
2. Pedophilic interests begin at adolescence	2. Pedophilic interests emerge in adulthood
3. No precipitating stress	3. Precipitating stress
4. Persistent interest — compulsive behavior	4. Involvements may be more episodic
5. Premeditated offenses	5. Less planning
6. Identification with the victim, and/or may adopt a pseudo-parental role to the victim	6. Replaces conflictual adult relationship with involvement with the child
7. Male victims are primary targets	7. Female victims are primary targets
8. Little or no sexual contact with agemates; is usually single or in marriage of convenience	8. Sexual contact with child co-exists with sexual contact with agemates; is usually married
9. Infrequent alcohol or drug-abuse	9. More frequent alcohol or drug abuse
10. Characterological immaturity; poor peer relationships	10. More traditional lifestyle but underdeveloped peer relation-ships
11. Offense is maladaptive resolution of life issues	11. Offense is maladaptive attempt to cope with specific life stresses

(Source: Groth 1978.)

Table 1.3
Situational and Preferential Child Molester

Situational Child Molester			
	Regressed	**Morally Indiscriminate**	**Sexually Indiscriminate**	**Inadequate**
Characteristics	Poor coping skills	Uses people	Sexual experimentation	Social misfit
Motivation	Substitution	Why not?	Boredom	Insecurity and curiosity
Victim Criteria	Availability	Vulnerability and opportunity	New and different	Non-threatening
Method of Operation	Coercion	Lure, force, or manipulation	Involved in existing activity	Exploits size advantage

Preferential Child Molester		
	Seductive	**Introverted**	**Sadistic**
Characteristics		Sexual preference for children; collects child pornography or erotica	
Motivation	Identification	Fear of communication	Need to inflict pain
Victim Criteria	Age and gender preferences	Strangers or very young	Age and gender preferences
Method of Operation	Seduction	Nonverbal sexual contact	Lure or force

(Source: Dietz 1983.)

Table 1.4. Pedophile Typology

Axis 2		Axis 1			
		High Fixation		Low Fixation (Regressed)	
		Low Social Competence	High Social Competence	Low Social Competence	High Social Competence
High Amount of Contact	Meaning of Contact: Interpersonal				
	Meaning of Contact: Narcissistic				
Low Amount of Contact	Low Physical Injury — Nonsadistic: Exploitative				
	Low Physical Injury — Sadistic: Muted				
	High Physical Injury — Nonsadistic				
	High Physical Injury — Sadistic				

*Adapted from Knight and Prentky, 1990.

is not aimed at understanding *why* child molesters have sex with children (treatment focus) but at recognizing and evaluating *how* child molesters have sex with children (prosecution focus). This can be of practical use to law enforcement.

An encouraging development in sex offender typologies is the work of Knight and Prentky (1990) who are developing and validating a sex offender classification system derived from intensive clinical observation of 460 offenders with more than 1400 variables (see Table 1.4).

They have developed a two-axis system of classifying pedophiles based on five dimensions. The first diagnostic dimension (Axis 1) is to determine the degree of fixation (Groth's fixated/regressed dichotomy) or the extent of pedophilic interest. This refers to the extent to which children are the major focus of the offender's thinking and fantasies. The second dimension (also on Axis 1) is the degree of social competence. This refers to the offender's success in employment, adult relationships, and social responsibilities.

The third dimension (the first variable on Axis 2) addresses the amount of contact the offender has with children, and, secondly, the nature of that contact. A high amount of contact with children would include both sexual and nonsexual contact in multiple contexts. The nature of the contact (the second variable on Axis 2) can range from interpersonal, narcissistic, high physical injury, and low physical injury. An offender with a high degree of contact with children who attempts to establish interpersonal (not exclusively sexual) relationships with children and where the aim of the offense is nonorgasmic is referred to as an **interpersonal** offender. The **narcissistic** offender also has a lot of contact with children but is less interested in establishing relationships with them. Most of the contact is sexual, and the focus of the offending behavior is orgasmic or phallic. In instances where the offender has infrequent contact with children, an assessment is made of the extent of the injury inflicted on the victims along with the extent to which sadistic fantasies are present. In some instances there may be little or no injury or only pushing, slapping, holding or threats. Among offenders with little contact with children and who inflict little or no physical injury on the victim, a distinction is made between those who report no sadistic fantasies accompanying the offenses (**exploitative**) and those whose offenses are motivated in part by **muted sadistic** fantasies, e.g., bondage, urination, spanking, or peculiar acts. Within the high injury group the sadistic/nonsadistic distinction is made on the basis of evidence that the aggression is eroticized. For example, the presence of violent sexualized fantasies, ritualized behavior, bizarre or peculiar sexual acts, or indications that the offender was aroused by seeing the victim in pain would lead to a **sadistic** assignment as opposed to a **nonsadistic, aggressive** decision.

Crossing the two axes of the Knight and Prentky typology results in 24 groups of pedophiles. Research on this typology is still in the preliminary stages, but there is evidence of the usefulness of 14 of the 24 possible types.

Consider the case of a man convicted of fondling a preschool male child. The man owns the daycare facility where the child was molested. He fantasizes a lot about children. He admits that seeing children in many different situations catches his attention and triggers sexual fantasies. Children love to be with him, because he is so engaging and seems to have a knack for relating to them. This man is outgoing, well respected in his community, and he volunteers for civic activities that focus on children. According to Knight and Prentky's schema, he would probably be classified as highly fixated, socially competent, and an interpersonal offender. He would be classified as an interpersonal offender as opposed to a narcissistic one because the offense in this instance was limited to fondling and because he has many contacts with children that are nonsexual.

Sexual Assault Offenders

Working with an incarcerated population of sex offenders, Groth (1979) observed that in every act of rape, both aggression and sexuality are involved but sexuality becomes the means of expressing the aggressive feelings that underlie the assault. He distinguished among three kinds of rapists.

The **anger** rapist uses sex to discharge feelings of pent-up anger and rage. Much more force is used than necessary to subdue the victim, and the source of that anger is often from other conflicts in his life. A high percentage of these offenders are acquainted with their victims. They comprise about one-third of the incarcerated sex offenders.

> "I was sitting there talking to this woman when all of a sudden I felt anger and rage inside of me. I lost control and struck out with violence. After the assault I felt relieved. I felt I had gotten even. There wasn't much sexual satisfaction; in fact, I felt a little disgusted. For a while thereafter the tension was relieved, but then it would start to build up again. Little things would upset me, and I couldn't shake them off" (Groth 1979).

The **power** rapist sexually assaults his victims to compensate for feelings of inadequacy. He uses intimidation and threats but the amount of physical injury is usually minimal. This is probably the most common group of incarcerated sex offenders, according to Groth. Their crimes are preceded by a lot of planning, rehearsing, and fantasizing. Control, mastery, and strength issues are paramount for these offenders. The power-assertive subtype tends to exploit his victims rather than inflict physical injury. The power-reassurance offender imagines that once a woman experiences his sexual prowess, she will think better of him. This kind of offender may return to earlier victims hoping that they will feel positively towards him.

> "I'd think about picking up a girl in a parking lot and imagine that when I accosted her, she would tell me I didn't need to force her. She would be eager to have sex with me and might even almost attack me ---- perhaps just my appearance or whatever would just turn her on, and she would rape me as if I were just what she had been hoping for" (Groth 1979).

For the **sadistic** rapist there is a sexual transformation of anger and power so that aggression itself becomes eroticized. That is, he finds the intentional maltreatment of his victim intensely gratifying and takes pleasure in the victim's torment, anguish, distress, and suffering. The assault usually involves bondage and torture and frequently has a bizarre or ritualistic quality to it. Explicitly abusive acts, such as biting, burning the victim with cigarettes, and whippings, are common. Sexual areas of the victim's body become a specific focus of injury and abuse. In some cases, the rape may not involve the offender's sexual organs. Instead, maybe used some type of instrument or foreign object such as a stick or bottle to penetrate the victim sexually. These offenses are also preceded by considerable fantasizing. Groth noted that these offenders make up about 5-6 percent of incarcerated sex offenders.

Knight and Prentky (1990) have developed a typology that underscores the diversity in the motivations for sexual assault (see Table 1.5). They identify four primary motivations for sexual assault: opportunity, pervasive anger, sexual gratification, and vindictiveness. These four motivational components appear related to enduring behavioral patterns that distinguish particular groups of offenders. For the **opportunistic** types the sexual assault appears to be an impulsive, typically unplanned, predatory act, con-

Table 1.5. Rapist Typology

Opportunity		Pervasively Angry	Sexual				Vindictive	
			Sadistic		Nonsadistic			
High SC*	Low SC		Overt	High SC/Muted	High SC	Low SC	Low SC	Moderate SC
Type 1	Type 2	Type 3	Type 4	Type 5	Type 6	Type 7	Type 8	Type 9

*SC = Social competence
Adapted from Knight and Prentky, 1990.

trolled more by what is happening in the offender's life at the moment than by long-term obsessions or fantasies. Assault for these persons is simply one among many instances of poor impulse control, as evidenced by their extensive history of unsocialized behavior in multiple domains. Their behavior suggests they are seeking immediate sexual gratification rather than an opportunity to release pent-up anger or frustration. They use only the force necessary to force the victim into submission.

The **pervasively angry** offenders, in contrast, readily resort to violence to gain access to their victims. In fact, violence may be used even in the absence of victim resistance. They often inflict serious physical injury on their victims, up to and including death. Although sexual assault is usually a part of the overall pattern for these offenders, their rage does not appear to be sexualized. They have extensive histories of problems in controlling aggression in many different situations. Their assaults are not usually driven by pre-existing fantasies.

Four types of rapists are characterized as having primarily "sexual" motivation. These offenders exhibit either protracted sexual or sadistic fantasies or preoccupations that motivate their sexual assaults and influence the way in which their offenses are executed. For all of these types some form of sexual preoccupation is a cardinal feature of their sexual assaults. Within the sexual types, two major subgroups can be distinguished on the basis of the presence or absence of sadistic fantasies or behaviors — the sadistic and nonsadistic groups. The two sadistic types show a frequent occurrence of erotic and destructive thoughts and fantasies. For the **overt sadistic sexual** type the aggression is manifested directly in physically damaging behavior in their sexual assaults. For the **muted sadistic sexual** type, the aggression is expressed either symbolically or through fantasy that is not acted out behaviorally. These two types of offenders correlate highly with low and high social competence respectively. The overt sadistic offenders appear to be angry and belligerent, who, except for their sadism and the greater planning of their sexual assaults, look similar to the pervasively angry types. The muted sadistic types, except for their sadistic fantasies and their slightly higher lifestyle impulsivity, resemble the high socially competent nonsadistic sexual type.

In the other two sexual types, the **nonsadistic sexual** types, the fantasies are less associated with violence and aggression than is characteristic of the sadistic types. Indeed, the two nonsadistic offender groups are thought to exhibit *less* interpersonal aggression in both sexual and nonsexual contexts than any of the other rapist types. When confronted by resistance from the victim, they are likely to flee rather than fight. Their fantasies and assault behaviors tend to reflect a composite of sexual arousal, distorted "male" attitudes about women and sex, and feelings of inadequacy about their sexuality and masculine self-image.

The **vindictive** types, the final motivational grouping, show a behavioral pattern that suggests that women are a central and exclusive focus of their anger. The assaults committed by these men are marked by behaviors that are physically harmful and appear to be intended to degrade and humiliate their victims. Yet, unlike the pervasively angry types, they show little or no evidence of undifferentiated anger, e.g., instigating fights with men. Although there is a sexual component in their assaults, there is no evidence that their aggression is eroticized as it is for the sadistic types, and no evidence that they are preoccupied with sadistic fantasies. In addition, like the nonsadistic sexual types, they differ from both the pervasively angry and overt sadistic types in their relatively lower level of lifestyle impulsivity.

The low social competence variants of the nonsadistic sexual and vindictive types (types 6 to 9) differ only in the amount of aggression in their assaults. Both of these groups are low substance abusing, low lifestyle impulsivity, socially isolated, and inadequate males. The **low social competence nonsadistic** type of offender appears to be preoccupied with sexual difficulties, and his rapes are suspected of being a distorted attempt to establish the sexual relationship he desires but is unable to attain. The **low social competence vindictive** type apparently responds to similar circumstances by becoming angry and punitive toward women and expressing his rage in his sexual assault.

Types 1 through 4 are all characterized by more lifestyle impulsivity, high unsocialized aggression, and more antisocial behavior.

What is apparent from this brief review of offender typologies is that sex offenders are a diverse group. Trying to categorize them in one or two groups is likely to distort and oversimplify what in reality is a complex interaction of many factors.

In addition to dispelling myths and misconceptions about the sex offender, construction of adequate typologies of offenders could have other desirable benefits. First, it could help to determine appropriate treatment modalities. Secondly, crucial events that precede and occur during the offenses could be identified and distinguish offenders with respect of outcome. Thirdly, judicial decision making could be facilitated on such issues as recidivism, dangerousness, release dispositions, and other factors.

Intellectually Disabled Sex Offenders

Most of the early reports as well as later reports — on incidence rates of sex offenders who are intellectually disabled report rates in the 10-15 percent range (Murphy et al. 1983). This is higher than expected, given the fact that intellectually disabled persons comprise 9 percent of the general population. These small reported differences may be spurious, however, because the limited social skills and cognitive abilities may make this kind of offender more likely to be apprehended. Most of the offenders in this group fall in the borderline (IQ 71 to 84) to mild retardation (IQ 55 to 70) range.

In our society, intellectually disabled persons are generally considered undervalued, disempowered, and socially isolated. They may be perceived as "holy innocents" — asexual persons — or, conversely, oversexed and dangerous. In a society conditioned to punishment rather than remediation, inappropriate or aggressive sexual behavior by this population invites, with few exceptions, the most negative systemic responses, ranging from harsh sentences to neglecting the seriousness of the behavior. Offenses committed by intellectually disabled sex offenders generally parallel those of nondisabled offenders, though their *modus operandi* (MO) may differ. Disabled or not, the sex offender should be held responsible for his behavior and be provided access to a continuum of specialized remedial interventions.

Despite some public pessimism, many specialized treatment providers agree that intellectually disabled sex offenders, particularly those identified as being in the borderline range of intellectual functioning, are surprisingly amenable to treatment. Intellectually disabled sex offenders who are diagnosed as *low risk* can usually benefit from treatment in specialized, individualized programs in the community (see Chapter 4). *Moderate- to high-risk* offenders, on the other hand, require longer term, highly structured, residential programs. The working guidelines and data sources used to assess risk for nondisabled offenders are generally useful for assessing disabled clients. Some risk issues, however, need to be considered differentially in assessing disabled and nondisabled offenders (Haven et al. 1990).

Impulsivity. The intellectually disabled sex offender's life may be characterized by an even greater degree of impulsivity than the nondisabled offender's because internal controls may be lacking. He is less able to project into the future or to understand the consequences of his actions. Many of the things that influence him are external. He may feel frustrated and powerless, unable to control what is happening to him. He may be quick to anger, and, lacking verbal and social skills, have fewer ways to cope

with his environment or divert his anger through emotional release. A high degree of impulsive behavior in the client's nonsexual history may heighten his risk of offending sexually.

Predatory Behavior. Compared to nondisabled sex offenders, intellectually disabled offenders tend to be less *covertly* predatory. Their offenses may not be substantially different from those
committed by nondisabled offenders except that they seldom establish consistent relationships with their victims. They seldom
have specific age, gender, or appearance preferences. In some
cases, they may grab a vulnerable victim on impulse. Consequently, it may be more difficult to predict which "high-risk"
situations or specific age or gender group might trigger this type
of offender's sexually aggressive behavior, placing him at higher
risk for reoffending.

Use of Physical Force or Weapons. It is important to
evaluate the type and degree of violence used in the commission
of the sexual assault. Offenders using **expressive** violence in the
commission of the crime exhibit the highest risk for reoffending
because the violence is intentional. The injury is inflicted because
it is a part of the offender's arousal pattern, not because it was
needed to gain the victim's compliance. **Instrumental** violence,
on the other hand, is characteristic of offenders who have lost
control and use violence or the threat of it to ensure compliance.
The intellectually disabled sex offender is more likely to use instrumental violence, in part because due to a lack the verbal skills
of coaxing, bribing, and manipulating, and in part because of the
low tolerance for frustration and tendency to panic in new situations.

Chronic Substance Abuse. Chronic substance abuse accen-
tuates the lack of control characteristic of many intellectually disabled offenders, placing them at higher risk for reoffending.

Firesetting, Animal Torture, and Eneuresis. The tendency for acting out aggressively appears to increase dramatically

with intellectually disabled sex offenders whose histories contain a combination of firesetting, animal torture, and bedwetting.

Prior Specialized Treatment Failure. Any offender who reoffends during or after completing a specialized sex offender treatment program is considered a higher risk. However, with intellectually disabled sex offenders, the *quality* of previous treatment should be first explored before automatically assuming the offender presents a higher risk to community safety. Prior treatment may have been inappropriate to the client's needs. Instead of automatically remanding such an offender to an institutional setting, consideration might be given to probation/parole with more restrictive and intrusive monitoring and intensive community programming.

Female Sex Offenders

Until recently, there has not been much research done on female sex offenders (Mayer 1992). Existing research focuses on the prevalence of sexual abuse by women, the characteristics of women who rape, and those who sexually abuse their children.

The prevalence of sexual abuse by women is an issue of debate and the data inconclusive. One of the difficulties in getting good data is that the sexual offenses committed by women are more incestuous or perpetrated against acquaintances. Children and acquaintances are less likely to report such incidents of victimization.

Female perpetrators are more likely than their male counterparts to self-report their crimes and to accept responsibility for what they did. Rather than minimizing their responsibility and the impact of their behavior, most express remorse and sadness. Some women commit sex crimes entirely on their own. Others get started with a male partner, but subsequently continue on their own. In still other instances, the sex crimes of women are male coerced. Women sexually abuse children more often than they victimize adults. The sex of the victims may not matter in that many female sex offenders abuse both boys and girls. The sexual acts committed run the gamut of those perpetrated by men against their victims.

When asked to explain why they sexually abused their victims, female sex offenders report such factors as prior ongoing abuse, being "used" by men, dependency on men, and rejection by men. Those who are coerced by their husbands or boyfriends report dependency, fear, threats, and physical abuse as reasons for their involvement.

Most female sex offenders who initiate some of the abuse they perpetrated admit being sexually aroused by their victims and by their sexual fantasies of their victims. Of women who abused only when male coerced, few of them admit to sexual arousal or fantasies.

> "I was sexually abused as a child from quite young on up, until I was a teenager. Some of the same things that I did to my children, some of the inappropriate boundaries, of growing up, of thinking, came from the family" (Matthews et al. 1989)

Most female sex offenders have been sexually victimized as children. They often come from very dysfunctional families where discipline is harsh and arbitrary. They often are alienated from family members throughout their lives. Their peer relationships as children are often inadequate too. Teased and bullied, they often lead lonely lives. Feeling inferior, they find self-destructive ways to be significant: promiscuity and chemical abuse.

Typology. The research on classifying female sex offenders is sparse and usually based on inadequate sample sizes. What follows must be viewed only as a tentative first attempt at understanding the diversity in the patterns of female sex offenders.

Some women who initiate the sexual activity with minors primarily choose victims who are not their own children. Many of their victims are teenagers, and they perceive themselves to be in a **teacher/lover** role. These women may be more inclined to minimize their behavior than other female offenders. Usually, they bear little animosity toward the children with whom they have been involved. They see themselves as teachers and, in some instances, as lovers of the adolescent victim. These offenders are likely to have been victimized in many different ways in their lives. They probably have a history of antisocial behavior in other respects. Chemical abuse is common among these offenders.

Another group of female sex offenders is the **predisposed (intergenerational)** group. These offenders usually act alone in initiating the sexual abuse. Their victims are most likely to be family members, especially their own children. Some of these women may have begun sexually offending as adolescents in babysitting situations. These women frequently come from extended families in which sexual abuse has been present for years. These women report being sexually abused at an early age, usually by more than one family member. They report being unable to get away from their abusive family relationships during adolescence, and they found it difficult to establish positive relationships with male peers. They were often exploited sexually in those relationships and gained reputations among their peers as being "easy." Many say that they did not enjoy these early sexual experiences but considered them instrumental to gaining the kind of acceptance they craved. These women are apt to lash out and hurt those around them, even as children. Substance abuse is common, as is compulsive eating. Their relationship histories are marked by unhealthy and dangerous pairings. They tend to have low self-esteem and are extremely dependent and nonassertive.

The third group of female sex offenders is the **male coerced**. These women are passive and feel powerless in interpersonal relationships. They tend to endorse a traditional lifestyle wherein the husband is the breadwinner and the wife is the homemaker. Most of these women marry young and have limited work histories. A history of childhood sexual victimization is common. Usually, the man becomes involved in sexual abuse first and brings the woman into it.

The final group is the **severely psychologically disturbed** abuser. In these offenders, there is usually a history of psychological problems such as depression, suicide attempts, peer problems, going back to adolescence or conduct disorders developing into antisocial behaviors during adulthood.

Are Sex Offenders Mentally Ill?

There seems to be a lot of confusion in peoples' minds about what causes a person to commit sex offenses. Most of us find such behavior so distasteful that we cannot imagine someone resorting to such perverse behavior. That is why it is sometimes tempting to conclude that anyone who does such a thing must be "mentally ill." In actuality, most estimates of the percent of sex offenders who have psychotic illnesses, such as schizophrenia, manic-depression, or organic brain syndromes, range from 5-8 percent. When supervising a sex offender with a severe psychological disturbance, recommend that a complete psychiatric work-up be conducted on the client. During that evaluation the person's need for medication will be considered and a schedule for medical supervision determined. Patients with severe psychological disorders cannot be counted on to comply with the medical regimen prescribed for them. Some believe they do not need the medication, others simply forget to take it, and still others resist taking the medication because of the side effects associated with it. The supervising officer should try to determine whether the offender is taking his or her medication as prescribed. A useful reference to consult regarding the various kinds of drugs likely to be prescribed for psychological disorders, the symptoms they are designed to treat, and the associated side effects is the *Physician's Desk Reference.*

More common than severely disturbed offenders are sex offenders who have long histories of poor impulse control and antisocial behavior that date back to their early teen years. They have difficulty in their social relationships, have been disruptive and truant in school, form few lasting friendships, feel minimal guilt, and, as a result, often commit many acts that are against the law or violate community standards. Sexual assault is merely one way of acting out for these persons. Offenders with this kind of history are said to have **antisocial** personalities. The hallmark of such individuals is the pervasiveness of their antisocial behavior. Moreover, their opportunistic nature leads to their committing sexually aggressive crimes during the course of other antisocial acts, such as burglary or robbery. Probably these offenders account for less than a third of the people who are charged with sex crimes.

Unlike those described as mentally ill or antisocial sex offenders, **paraphiliacs** usually commit a sexual offense because they have what is referred to in psychiatric terms as a *paraphilia.* This group of offenders differs from the prior two groups because of their characteristic *obsessive thoughts and compulsive urges to carry out sexually aggressive behaviors.* They may in almost every other respect be indistinguishable from other men or women. It is just in this one area of their behavior that they appear unable to exercise consistent control. Offenders of this type may be executives, college professors, police officers, or even probation and parole officers! Some offenders may experience a paraphilia during a time of extraordinary stress such as illness, injury, relationship problems, or financial difficulties.

Multiple Paraphilias

It is common for sex offenders to engage in different types of paraphilias. For example, a person may start his or her assaultive patterns with "hands-off" behaviors such as exhibitionism, voyeurism, obscene phone calls, or frottage. Abel reported that over 50 percent of the rapists treated in his program had also engaged in pedophilia and just under 30 percent had engaged in exhibitionism. Another 20 percent had practiced voyeurism. Among child molesters just under 30 percent had exhibited themselves and 17 percent had committed rape. Approximately 50 percent of the men in the study had multiple deviant acts.

Treatment or Punishment?

The public reaction to sex crimes is usually severe and that most people believe these offenders should be imprisoned in order to both protect the public and punish the offender. In fact, however, most persons convicted of sex offenses are given probation. Yet, supervision following the imposition of criminal sanctions is unlikely in the majority of instances to be sufficient to insure that the person convicted of a sex crime will not reoffend. If the risk of reoffending is going to be reduced, the offender should be mandated to participate in a specialized treatment program for sex offenders.

As for those who are sent to prison, it is clear that the majority of them will be released at some point. Without specialized treatment programs in prison and follow-up community-based programs, the prison experience may only increase the offender's pathology so that they come out with worse fantasies then when they went in. More violent and angry than when they were sent to prison, their crimes may escalate so that more harm is done to their victims following release. Disposing of sex offender cases with an emphasis on punishment and incarceration to the exclusion of treatment may only reinforce the offender's shame and guilt. Ironically, the offensive behaviors stem from these very elements.

Punishment without treatment only serves to feed the offender's isolation, while the offender reinforces deviant fantasies through masturbation during the jail or prison sentence. On the other hand, legal constraints on the behavior of sex offenders are frequently needed to encourage their continued treatment participation.

Can Sex Offenders Change?

The answer to the question about the likelihood of sex offenders effectively changing their behavior depends upon what is implied by the inquiry. Can significant reductions be achieved in reoffense rates of sex offenders? The answer, based on preliminary evaluation and follow-up studies of various kinds of sex offender treatment programs, suggests that this is a reasonable expectation. If, on the other hand, the question is, "Can sex offenders be 'cured'?" the answer has to be qualified. Most sex-offender treatment specialists view the offender as vulnerable to his deviant sexual preference indefinitely. The key word is not "cure" but "self-control." There seems to be a parallel between sex offenders and persons involved in other long-term addictive and compulsive patterns of behavior. We do not refer to "ex-alcoholics" but about alcoholics who maintain their sobriety. In the same way, we talk about sex offenders who do not offend anymore.

Effective treatment programs for sex offenders depend on competent and thorough assessment and screening of applicants, multimodal strategies that are tailored to each offender, sufficient duration (intensity) for the treatment to be effective, and relapse prevention training. Caution needs to be exercised, however, so that treatment is not oversold. The reality is that there are some sex offenders for whom present-day treatment techniques have not been shown to be very effective. This is true for very violent or sadistic offenders, pedophiles who target male children, and exhibitionists. It is also true that some offenders do not want to deal with their problems. They have found their sexual preoccupations to be pleasurable and may not be willing to give them up. Nevertheless, sex offenders should be provided the opportunities to learn the appropriate and necessary skills and tools to control their behaviors if they want to do so.

2
The Origins of Sexual Offending

Men often seem preoccupied with promoting self-interest in the areas of sex and aggression. Learning to control these biologically based aggressive tendencies occurs through our growing-up experiences in the world. Despite that human males are capable of using aggression, threats, or coercion in a sexual context, not all men do so. Though, clearly, all men are physically capable of molesting children, only few do. The biological capacity to enact certain behaviors does not mean that the display of these behaviors should be accepted as inevitable, nor should we excuse someone for engaging in them. Biological endowment should be seen as setting the stage for learning, providing limits and possibilities rather than determining outcomes. Indeed, in the case of sexual offending, the contribution of biological factors may be minimal once learning has established patterns of behavior.

Biological Influences

The task of disentangling aggression and sex would be easier if these processes were less interconnected. Both aggression and sex seem to be mediated by the same neural sites which predominantly involve midbrain structures such as the hypothalamus, septum, hippocampus, amygdala, and preoptic area. The neural networks within these areas appear to be remarkably similar for sex and aggression. Additionally, the same endocrines, namely the sex steroids, activate both sex and aggression.

These activating effects appear to be minimal prior to adolescence, but once puberty begins, hormonal levels increase fourfold within the first 10 months, reaching adult levels after a mere two years (Marshall and Barbaree 1990). This is also the time when dramatic increases occur in both sexual and aggressive behaviors. Puberty and the ensuing early years of adolescence are, therefore, likely to be important times for learning to express and channel sex and aggression. It may be that readiness to learn sexual behaviors and preferences declines after adolescence in the same way that other mammals exhibit critical periods for learning specific kinds of behaviors. If puberty does constitute a critical period for the development of enduring sexual preferences, and if the same biological activators underlie aggression, we may reasonably assume that the same is true of aggressive behavior. However, the biological factors mediating sex and aggression may not be the same for all individuals. Having unusually high levels of sex steroids may make the task of acquiring inhibitions against sexual aggression more difficult.

Research results have not demonstrated reliable differences in the testosterone levels of convicted rapists and nonrapists; but higher levels have been found in those offenders who were markedly aggressive or sadistic in their sexual assaults (Rada et al. 1976). Among rapists, then, there may be a small percentage who are driven by chronically high hormonal levels, but the majority simply appear not to have acquired sufficiently strong inhibitory controls over sex and aggression. There do not appear to be comparable studies of exhibitionists or child molesters.

Biological factors present the adolescent male with the task of learning to appropriately separate sex and aggression, and to inhibit aggression in a sexual context. Although our biological heritage can make these tasks difficult, developmental and other environmental factors appear to play the most important role in shaping the expression of sexual needs and in controlling aggression.

The attitudes and behaviors acquired during childhood set the stage for how the developing male responds to the sudden onset of strong desires characteristic of pubescence. They determine whether the individual will respond with a prosocial or an antisocial mental set. These mental sets will be strongly influenced at this time by the sociocultural attitudes expressed by the society at large, and these influences may remain as important factors throughout the individual's life. Similarly, certain circumstances can render ineffective even rather well-entrenched social controls, such that sexually offensive tendencies can be released in otherwise prosocial males.

Childhood Experiences

Early developmental experiences of boys who later become sex offenders may not prepare them for the biological changes that occur at puberty and the associated desire to engage in sex and aggression. Poor socialization, particularly a violent parenting style, will both facilitate the use of aggression and hinder the youth's access to more appropriate sociosexual interactions. These unfortunate influences may also instill a serious lack of confidence in the growing boy as well as strong feelings of resentment and hostility. These feelings of ineptitude will certainly not help the pubescent male acquire appropriate inhibitory controls over sex and aggression; to the contrary, they may serve to reinforce just the opposite dispositions.

Parents

The family backgrounds of rapists and the parental training practices to which they are typically exposed as children are illuminating. The early home life of boys who later become sex offenders is often characterized by violence and sexual abuse. The children are punished frequently and severely in a manner which is inconsistent and rarely functionally related to their behavior. The mothers and fathers of rapists are often both inferior parents with whom the children do not identify. The fathers are frequently aggressive, drunken, and in trouble with the law. Given the hostile home environment, it is not surprising to learn that many of these children engage in antisocial behavior before adulthood, which, in turn, makes it more likely that they will exhibit further antisocial behavior as adults.

That these children grow into insensitive adults who are concerned primarily with their own interests and needs is hardly surprising. Modeling the behavior of their parents, we would expect them to be aggressive and to take whatever they want without regard for the rights of others. Similarly, we would expect them to learn to use aggression as a way of solving problems and securing what they want.

Young boys prepared by a loving family for the hormonal changes of puberty, provided continued and consistent encouragement for prosocial behavior, should be able to make the transition to adult functioning with both the social constraints against aggression in place and the skills necessary to develop effective relationships. For children who come from the kind of disruptive backgrounds described above, however, the pubertal release of hormones may serve to fuse sex and aggression, enhance already acquired aggressive tendencies, and lead to a failure to develop sufficiently strong inhibitions against the expression of sex in a violent context.

Discipline

Severe and inconsistent punishment produces emotional indifference in children; but more importantly, it also produces oppositional behavior (Wahler 1969). It is children's oppositional behavior in that is predictive of a criminal and self-centered orientation in adulthood. Such oppositional behavior in adult offenders is understood to be expressed not only in unfeeling and criminal behavior but also in a readiness to respond with anger and aggression toward others (Schmauk 1970).

Loneliness

Two of the most important outcomes for male socialization from appropriate parenting are development of self-confidence and a strong emotional attachment to others. In dysfunctional families the realization of these outcomes is seriously compromised and later limits the offender's ability to develop strong and positive attachment bonds. This may further alienate the offender and cause him to experience emotional loneliness. Loneliness has been shown to be highly related to hostility and aggression (Check and Marshall 1990), so that this failure to develop the capacity for intimacy may be expected to result in aggressive behavior, especially in a sexual context.

Lacking the interpersonal skills necessary to interact effectively with females of his own age may lead to anxiety when confronted with such occasions. Feelings of masculine inadequacy and even anger toward women may be apparent because they may be seen as the source of these problems. Social inadequacy cannot only increase stress and anxiety but lower inhibitions against sexual aggression as well.

Masturbatory Fantasies

Masturbatory activity among males is usually accompanied by arousing fantasies. Some young boys, who feel cut off from female company, may develop fantasies which satisfy their need to see themselves as masculine. These fantasies may borrow from media messages wherein "maleness" is all too often identified with power, control, and either an indifference to or a contempt for women. Such fantasies may evolve into scenes of rape, or exhibitionism, or sex with younger, more vulnerable persons.

Other sources of autoerotic fantasies include early exploratory sexual activity, witnessing others' sexual activity (in person or through various media), and verbal accounts of others' sexual exploits. Minor variations of the original fantasy successively substituted for the original one (perhaps to avoid boredom) and paired with masturbation can elicit high sexual arousal plus orgasm. For example, having acquired sexual responses to adult females, a male may gradually introduce elements of youthfulness into his imagined partner during masturbation. Over successive occasions he may progress to imagining unacceptably young partners while masturbating and these fantasies along with the accompanying sexual arousal will entrench a deviant sexual attraction. The young boy not only learns deviant sexual scripts as behavioral possibilities, he may also come to view himself differently from other boys and increase his sense of estrangement from peers (Law and Marshell 1990).

During masturbation the pairing of the powerful erotic physical stimulation with sexual fantasy permits many elements of that fantasy, both sexual and nonsexual, to become eroticized, i.e., sexually stimulating. A person with a brief history of pedophilic behavior might, in masturbation, focus on either real or idealized aspects of an actual or potential victim. At first the focus might be on general features, such as the victim's looks, small stature, or overall shape of the body. By selectively focusing on more specific aspects of the victim with potential erotic features, such as size of the penis, shape of the buttocks, absence of pubic hair, these features may become stronger cues to sexual arousal than the original, more general ones (Laws and Marshell 1990).

Sociocultural Context

Given the difficulties involved in acquiring the necessary inhibitions over sex and aggression, and the often misleading messages our society conveys to youths, it is a little surprising that most people do learn to demonstrate appropriate behavioral restraint. During childhood the influence of parents may be primary but, as the child grows up, the factors outside the family become progressively more important. Those who by their family upbringing have been left poorly prepared to function effectively will seize on those messages that serve their needs. Boys with low self-esteem will often be attracted to those attitudes and behaviors which confer on them a sense of power rather than those emphasizing cooperation and equality.

Studies of Western societies have shown that acceptance of male dominance by men is associated with negative attitudes toward women, an acceptance of rape myths, and either having raped or an admission by the man that he would rape if he could be sure of escaping detection (Malamuth and Check 1981). Also, males who have a strong need for dominance are more accepting of rape and tend to downplay the aggressive elements of sexual assault (Stewart and Sokol 1997).

Availability of Pornography

The role of pornography in the commission of sex crimes is controversial. The U.S. Commission on Obscenity and Pornography (1970) claimed there was no evidence to indicate that pornography is harmful. However, it is inconsistent to claim that pornographic images exert no influence while claiming that advertising images do. The problem, it seems, is to determine what influence pornography has and on whom rather than simply evaluating whether or not it has any influence.

Recent research has focused on pornographic displays of violent sex and sex with children and suggests that exposure made interpersonal violence against women more acceptable to normal males and also increased their acceptance of rape myths (Malamuth and Check 1981). Viewing violent pornography increases the subsequent aggression males display toward females (Donnerstein 1980), especially in already angered males (Gray 1982).

There is evidence that viewers become desensitized to violence after repeated exposures and that this effect particularly applies to sexual violence. Worse than this simple acquired tolerance of violence, however, is the threat that exposure to dehumanized violence toward women will lead to the commission of cruel and violent acts toward females.

No one expects every man who views pornography to subsequently rape a woman or molest a child. Interestingly, it has been found that men with restricted sexual socialization are more behaviorally affected by exposure to pornography than are males who have had a more normal upbringing (Fisher and Byrne 1978).

No one really understands how exposure to pornography affects sex offenders, but there is cursory information that shows that rapists and child molesters characteristically use pornography more frequently than do normal males, and one-third of the offenders report being incited to offend by viewing pornography (Marshall 1988).

Immediate Circumstances

Hormonal factors and other internal states of sex offenders are insufficient to completely explain sex crimes, because offenders typically demonstrate adequate control of their acting-out tendencies until they perceive an opportunity to enact their desires without being caught. Clearly these people recognize, and are responsive to, the social rules that constrain other citizens. Something about the circumstances where they commit their offenses along with their own internal states at the time produce loss of control. It may well be that many of the circumstances that lead sex offenders to overcome their inhibitions against offending are deliberately created by offenders themselves but some may be externally induced as well. How vulnerable any one person is to these influences depends on that person's history.

One contributing factor commonly reported by sex offenders is excessive use of **alcohol** (although they may exaggerate their alcohol abuse as an excuse). Police and victim reports often confirm intoxication in as many as 70 percent of sexual assaults (Christo et al. 1979). Males who are normally inhibited by aggressive cues in the context of a sexual encounter often fail to be inhibited to the same degree by these cues when they are intoxicated (Barbaree et al. 1983).

Many rapists report feeling hostile toward females at the time of their sexual assaults. Laboratory-induced **anger** has been found to be associated with greater sexual arousal to forced sex among even normal males (Yates et al. 1984).

Other laboratory results demonstrate that **sexual arousal** prior to exposure to particular types of sexual stimuli also make men more accepting and responsive to forced sex (Malamuth et al. 1980). Prior arousal enhances responding to all subsequent sexual stimuli, but prior arousal induced by forced sex stimuli enhances arousal to the rape cues presented later. Many offenders report feeling sexually excited for an extended period of time before committing their offenses.

Information indicates sexual offending is an acceptable behavior may lower inhibitions against such behavior. This is significant in view of the fact that some forms of pornography which depict sexual offending both induce arousal and suggest that such behavior is acceptable.

Other transitory influences that have been suggested as possible sources of disinhibition, but which have not as yet been borne out by research, include anonymity and the reduced possibility of detection, such as in large urban settings, alienation from others which facilitates dehumanization of victims, stress, and anxiety (Marshall and Barbaree 1990).

Summary

All men have a capacity to sexually aggress which must be overcome by appropriate socialization experiences to instill social inhibitions toward such behavior. Variations in hormonal functioning may make this task more difficult for some. More importantly, however, is poor parenting, especially the use of inconsistent and harsh discipline in the absence of love. Such a history typically fails to instill these constraints and may even serve to facilitate the fusion of sex and aggression rather than separate these two tendencies. Attitudes derived from our society and culture may negatively interact with poor parenting to enhance the likelihood of sexual offending, if these cultural beliefs express traditional patriarchal views. The young male whose childhood experiences have ill-prepared him for a prosocial life may readily accept these views to bolster his sense of manliness. Whenever such a male gets intoxicated, angry, or feels stressed, and finds himself in circumstances where he is not known or thinks he can get away with offending, he is likely to sexually offend, especially if he is aroused at the time.

3
Assessing Treatment Approaches

Defining effective sex offender treatment is not always easy. Sometimes even deciding what "treatment" is can be confusing, because the word is used for any number of interventions in the mental health field. When applied to sex offenders it usually means any type of intervention designed to reduce the likelihood the offender will commit more sex offenses. Some people object to the term "treatment" to describe interventions for sex offenders because, as they point out, it implies that something akin to a disease is being treated, and the expectation is that the problem will be "cured." Such a view distorts the compulsive aspect of deviant sexual impulses, leading the offender to mistakenly assume that the problem is cured and no longer needs attention. This notion oversimplifies the difficulties encountered and the resources needed to prevent reoffending.

Overcoming Skepticism

Treatment for sex offenders has been an unpopular concept. Many people are so horrified when they hear the stories of victims and when newspaper headlines announce reoffenses by paroled sex offenders, they find it hard to believe these kinds of offenders can actually be helped. Indeed, it is difficult to understand how a person could molest a child or brutally assault a woman. In trying to make sense of such behavior it is tempting to resort to oversimplistic assessments and recommend punitive consequences — exclusive of treatment — for persons found guilty of sex crimes. Consistent with this view is the belief that sex offenders constitute too great a threat to public safety to risk returning them to the community. It has become increasingly clear, however, that most of these offenders will be free at some point to move about in society. Unless thoughtful efforts with proven effectiveness are introduced to address the problems presented by sex offenders, the likelihood of subsequent offending appears high.

Many experts are optimistic about treatment outcome while others are pessimistic. Close scrutiny of detractors suggests they often make one of three mistakes in their research. First, those who fail to find support for the effectiveness of sex offender treatment tend to base their conclusion on an all-or-nothing criterion; that is, all interventions should be effective with all offenders. Few treatment specialists maintain that this can be accomplished. Proponents of sex offender treatment measure effectiveness in terms of percentage points in reduced recidivism, not "cures" or 100 percent success rates.

Secondly, those researchers concluding that most treatment programs are ineffective often have a very loose definition of treatment. Should intensive supervision programs in probation or parole be considered treatment? What about one-session counseling interventions by police officers? Part of the difficulty in making sense of the research reviews of treatment effectiveness is that until recently it has been difficult to spell out what constitutes effective treatment for sex offenders.

The third area of disagreement between proponents and detractors of treatment effectiveness for sex offenders is that the latter group sometimes imposes such high standards for methodological rigor in evaluating treatment outcome that little is found to be worthwhile. Demanding the present literature to demonstrate unequivocally that treatment is effective across all types of offenders is to court certain disappointment. This is not to say that methodological considerations should be put aside (see Table 3.1). To the contrary, confidence in the findings of evaluative research must address such issues as sample size, type specifications of offenders treated, clear description of the treatment procedures used, and objective outcome data collected over at least a one-year post-treatment period (preferably five years). However, when a variety of outcome studies reveal subsequent reoffense rates substantially below that expected of similar but untreated offenders, then it seems reasonable to conclude that we are on the right track. This conclusion would not necessarily imply that all approaches to treatment, or even all applications of any particular approach, are effective.

The majority of sex-offender-treatment specialists believe that many sex offenders can be helped if • evaluation is competent, • placement is appropriate, • the treatment mode meets the needs of the offender, and • the offender wants to change.

One approach to sex-offender treatment would be to give every offender an opportunity to participate. If only those offenders who appear to be the "best" candidates for treatment are selected, only a small number of people will be admitted to the programs. In some institutional programs, only those judged to be most at risk for reoffending are selected for treatment. Where this is the case, outcome data will likely reflect less success. In other programs the selection criteria achieve the opposite goal; that is, the offenders least at risk enter treatment. Unfortunately, selection criteria are not always clear in published reports of program effectiveness. Those who advocate selectivity, especially for community-based programs, express cautious optimism about some treatment approaches for certain types of offenders. There are a lot of sex offenders for whom we do not know what to do, particularly the more violent ones. If we advocate broad selection

Table 3.1
Problems in Assessing Effectiveness of Treatment

1. Few evaluation studies used comparison groups of untreated offenders.

2. Reoffense rates are at least in part a function of whether the offender has a prior conviction. Few studies make this distinction in evaluating treatment effectiveness.

3. The selection criteria for entry into treatment are not always made clear.

4. Recidivism rates increase steadily over the full range of follow-up, however long that may have been, which makes comparisons across studies more difficult.

5. Reviews of treatment effectiveness often do not differentiate among different types of treatment; thus accounting for some of the variability in effectiveness outcomes.

6. Few evaluation studies acknowledge that marginally effective treatments might help one offender who would otherwise have reoffended and thereby spare one or more potential victims.

7. There are too few studies that attempt to calculate the differential costs in dollars to society if sex offenders are untreated and subsequently reoffend as opposed to their being treated and realizing lower reoffense rates.

8. Few studies present recidivism results separately for each offender type (e.g., homosexual versus heterosexual pedophile).

9. Offender classifications based on a single offense or conviction may be misleading.

10. The kinds of offenders who drop out of treatment must be carefully monitored and considered in evaluating treatment effectiveness.

criteria for including offenders in treatment programs, we may run the risk of overselling programs. That, in turn, could lead to doubt that anything works.

Although there are many questions about the effectiveness of sex-offender treatment which remain to be answered, there are some general conclusions that seem warranted at this time. There is a growing body of evidence suggesting some sex offenders can be effectively treated to reduce subsequent recidivism. Clearly, however, not all programs are successful and not all sex offenders profit from treatment. Comprehensive cognitive/behavioral programs and those programs which use anti-androgens in conjunction with psychological treatments seem to offer the greatest hope for effectiveness. The best of these programs are most effective with certain types of child molesters. Incest and heterosexual pedophiles seem to profit more than homosexual offenders do. The offenders most difficult to treat are men convicted of sexual assault.

What Is Good Sex-Offender Treatment?

A supervising officer, when faced with a court order for evaluation or treatment in a sex-offender case, is left with the problem of deciding whether the treatment available in his or her area is "good" sex-offender treatment.

Suppose you receive the following report from a therapist you have enlisted to treat a 28-year-old man who was convicted of molesting an 11-year-old boy in his neighborhood.

Dear Officer _____:

Over the past three months I have conducted individual psychotherapy with James _____ whom you referred to me in January of this year. He was cooperative and faithfully attended his sessions with me twice a month.

We talked at length about the stressors in his life over the past two years, and it is apparent that his coping ability had deteriorated considerably, leading eventually to the offense for which he was convicted. Some of these stressors included pressure at work, disappointment at being passed over for promotion, marital problems, and financial difficulties. Furthermore, James is estranged from his own parents and feels unaccepted by his in-laws. These problems have been a primary focus of treatment.

James denies ever having fondled children before the incident in question. Since his sexual involvement with the neighbor boy led to the only arrest in his life, and since he has had an apparently successful lifestyle, the incident with the boy was probably an isolated one, induced by the stressors in his life, and unlikely to be repeated. Moreover, his MMPI profile shows no indication of pathology.

James is embarrassed about the incident that led to his arrest and seems sincerely determined not to repeat his mistake. His vocational and marital problems seem to be much improved. Now that he has learned more effective ways of coping with stress, I believe he no longer needs treatment. Correspondingly, I believe his risk of reoffending is minimal.

Sincerely,
Joe E. Shrink

How should the officer evaluate the services this client received and how much confidence can the officer have in presenting these findings to the court? The services provided and the conclusions drawn by the provider in the above letter are insufficient because *effective sex-offender treatment must specifically address the client's aggression, sexual problems, and deviance.* If the therapist is not talking to the offender about these issues, the treatment does not satisfy court-ordered conditions, and it is probably not helping the offender resolve the problems underlying the offense.

Some offenders may claim they have received religious counseling from someone affiliated with a church, and since they have now "become right with the Lord," they are no longer in any danger of reoffending. Although pastoral counseling should not be discounted, the offender should be told that additional treatment, acceptable to the court and the supervising officer, will be required.

Because incidents like these are becoming increasingly common for probation and parole officers, it is important that you have some understanding of what constitutes specialized treatment for sex offenders.

Goals of Treatment

The pioneer sex-offender treatment programs were based primarily on the traditional medical or psychiatric model. At that time, the preferred forms of treatment involved one-to-one individual psychotherapy, plus group therapy led by one therapist who was usually a male. In contrast, today's specialized sex-offender assessment and treatment programs rarely diagnose offenders in conventional psychiatric terms or treat them by such traditional modes. Sex offenders are understood to require combinations of highly diverse treatment approaches tailored to address the offenders' patterns and perceived needs, reflective of the many issues surrounding the offenses (see Table 3.2). Few traditional training programs and curricula of schools of medicine, mental health, and social work offer programs and training for working with this population.

The growing consensus concerning effective sex-offender treatment favors an integrated approach incorporating psychodynamic, behavioral, cognitive, and biomedical elements, as well as a wide range of educational and training components (see Chapter 4).

Table 3.2
Goals of Treatment

To reduce recidivism through:

1. A complete, individualized assessment and treatment plan.

2. Enabling the offender to
    - accept responsibility for the offense(s) in which he or she has been involved
    - understand the sequence of thoughts, feelings, events, circumstances, and arousal stimuli that make up the "offense syndrome" that precedes his or her involvement in sexually aggressive behaviors

3. Teaching the offender to
    - intervene in or break into his or her offense pattern at its earliest stage
    - call upon appropriate methods, or procedures to suppress, control, manage, and stop the behavior chain

4. Engaging the offender in re-education and resocialization to
    - replace antisocial thoughts and behaviors with prosocial ones
    - acquire a positive self-concept and new attitudes and expectations for himself or herself
    - learn new social and sexual skills to cultivate positive, satisfying, pleasurable, and nonthreatening relationships with others

5. Providing the residential sex offender with opportunities to safely test his or her newly acquired insights and control mechanisms in the community without the risk of affronting or harming the wider community.

6. Providing postrelease support and access to therapeutic treatment to help him or her sustain therapeutic gains.

"We are obviously talking about an issue that is much broader than simply a clinical or a psychological issue. It is a cultural, a legal, a political, an economic, an educational, a medical, and a spiritual issue. And if we are going to be effective in combating this problem, it really means approaching it from all of these perspectives" (Groth 1983).

Assessment of the offender — a key element of any successful program — is an ongoing process, not just an initial part of treatment. At the end of residential treatment, postrelease treatment is an extension of the total treatment plan.

Expect Denial

Everyone who works with sex offenders should expect that most of these individuals will deny, at least in part, their involvement in sex crimes or their deviant sexual arousal (see Table 3.3). Clinical experience suggests offenders initially tell is only the "tip of the iceberg."

The most common type of denial is probably the **denial of planning and fantasy** before the offense. In this case offenders try to convince the examiner that it "just happened." Such a contention, however, is unconvincing, because accumulated evidence from working with sex offenders reveals that fantasy and planning are integral parts of the offense cycle. One way to respond to this kind of denial is to suggest that if the offender did not think about it ahead of time, if he did not fantasize, then he would have no way to intervene next time. Such a circumstance makes him too great a risk to be treated in the community. Instead, he should be incarcerated for as long as possible. Faced with that prospect, the offender may amazingly recover his memory!

Table 3.3
Types of Denial

Before the offense

- Denial of deviant fantasy
- Denial of planning
- During the offense

Denial of behavior

- Minimization of behavior
- Rationalization of behavior
- Denial of deviant behaviors
- Denial of responsibility

After the offense

- Denial of current problem
- Denial of difficulty of change
- Denial of possibility of relapse
- Denial of seriousness of effects

Another kind of denial is the **refusal to admit to the behavior** in question. The offender may appear outraged that such accusations would be made of him or her. A common ploy may be to cast doubt on the accusation by suggesting ulterior motives the victim or other significant person may have had in making the report. For example, a sexual assault victim may be accused by the alleged perpetrator of crying "rape" to cover up a sexual indiscretion from her boyfriend or husband, or a child victim may be said to have misinterpreted his intentions. An offender may further allege that the charges against him are trumped up to enable a former spouse to get custody of the child or limit visitation. Sometimes it is easy to be taken in by this kind of denial if it is made by someone who does not fit our stereotype of an offender, for example, a highly educated person with a good job who is married and appears to be sincere.

Another tack is to admit some aspect of the offense but not all of it. In other words, the strategy here is to **minimize** what took place. For example, an offender may admit to scratching his stepdaughter's back under her T-shirt and massaging her above and below her breasts, but never fondling her breast and never admitting to any sexual intent. Sometimes offenders also deny the length of time over which the molestation occurred in cases of pedophilia.

Some offenders will admit the sexual offense but **rationalize** it in terms of sex education or helping her overcome a previous victimization by showing her how sexual behavior can be gentle and soothing. Another way to rationalize the offense is to claim that the victim consented to the sexual encounter and only later cried "rape."

Some sex offenders will admit to the victim's account of the offense, but will **claim that this is the only time it ever happened.** This may occasionally be true, especially with adolescent offenders, but as was pointed out in the first chapter, many sex offenders have a history of undetected offenses. Additionally, offenders usually have a history of deviant sexual fantasies, of masturbating to the fantasy, of planning, and often of grooming, i.e., gaining the trust and cooperation, the victim.

Denial of responsibility is another common response among offenders who admit their offenses. "She behaved provocatively toward me." "She has a reputation for sleeping with anyone." "My wife encouraged me to get sex elsewhere, just as long as I left her alone." In treatment, sex offenders are often encouraged to explore what led them to offend. This kind of inquiry may actually encourage this kind of denial.

Some sex offenders may admit to the offense but **deny they currently have a problem.** They may excuse the earlier offense due to claims such as they were not thinking or because they had just lost their jobs and were under too much stress. Alternatively, the offender may say that the arrest and the prospect of imprisonment has made him realize the error, and it will never happen again. This kind of statement may actually reflect a drop in the offenders' sexual interest because of the anxiety and humiliation he experienced following discovery.

"I got away from God, and now that I've straightened out again, I'll be okay." Such a statement may reflect acknowledgment of the offense but a **denial of difficulty to change.** If he is an incest offender who was required to leave home, he may press to return home within a week or two.

Related to the above denial is **overconfidence about the possibility of relapse.** Frequently, these offenders live only in the present and fail to see beyond their current state of mind. When subsequently presented with another opportunity and the urge to commit another offense, they may again only be able to focus on their present state of mind and be unable to resist reoffending.

Many offenders try to trivialize their behavior by **denying that the offenses had any lasting impact.** This kind of denial reflects a profound failure of empathy, and this lack of empathy is a good predictor of reoffending. If the offense was of so little consequence to the victim, there can be little harm in doing it again.

Assessment

A psychosexual evaluation, if requested, should be done at the same time as the presentence investigation — after a conviction — particularly if the offender is in denial. The presence of a deviant arousal pattern in a denying incest offender provides clear evidence for the court that the offender is not a "situational" offender and may be a serious reoffending risk.

There is not a test or interview technique that will elicit information on sexual deviancy in the presence of denial. A denying offender will simply fabricate a nondeviant background and deny any thoughts, feelings, fantasies, or behavior he feels are not "normal." However, careful interviewing, confrontation with the results of a plethysmograph, and with the consequences of denial may enable an offender who has previously denied his offense to admit it and thus take the first step towards accountability.

Occasionally, a psychosexual evaluation will be requested on an admitting offender for the purposes of plea bargaining. The state's attorney may want to know whether the offender has a deviant arousal pattern, whether he has a long or a short history of sexual offending, whether he is sexually aroused to violence, or other indicators, before agreeing to a particular plea bargain.

In the case of a denying offender, however, the psychosexual evaluation must be done after the trial. Once the offender has been convicted, the examiner can properly refuse to discuss the offender's guilt or innocence, insisting instead that the issue has already been settled by the courts. She or he can state flatly that denial of the offense simply means the offender is not willing to take responsibility for the offense and thus is doubly dangerous.

Before the trial the offender may believe that denial is in his best interest. After the trial, the examiner can make it clear that it is not. Thus, the offender has some reason to be cooperative, while before he did not.

When mental health professionals are asked to evaluate sex offenders, they often employ the procedures customarily used to assess persons who are depressed or anxious. Accordingly, a standard battery of tests may be used. One aspect of such an assessment would be to give an intelligence test. What purpose would this measurement serve? There are sex offenders who are brilliant and others who are retarded, so how does knowing an offender's IQ serve treatment decisions? Perhaps an IQ test might be appropriate in assessing a sex offender if there is some question about whether the person is retarded or whether there was some other problem such as a learning disability or anxiety. In the case of a retarded offender, such information would be useful in establishing an appropriate level of treatment.

Projective techniques, such as the Rorschach and Thematic Apperception Test (TAT), are often a part of a psychologist's assessment battery. These instruments are thought to have the advantage of circumventing conscious attempts to mislead the examiner. However, their primary purpose is to uncover intrapsychic processes or personality traits. This kind of information is of limited value in evaluating sex offenders, because these characteristics have little to do with sexual deviancy. Although projective techniques may reveal whether or not a person is depressed or obsessive-compulsive, they are unlikely to reveal whether a person is guilty of a sex offense or even deviant sexual arousal. In other words, these measures will not distinguish offenders from non-offenders.

The Bender-Gestalt Test requires the examinee to reproduce standardized drawings. It is thought to be a measure of neurological dysfunction and/or impulsivity, i.e., acting without carefully considering the consequences of such actions. Sex offenders, however, are rarely impulsive. Child molesters carefully groom children, and men who sexually assault women often take considerable precautions against getting caught.

If these typical kinds of assessment instruments are less than helpful in assessing sex offenders, what should be the focus and means of evaluating these people? Salter has listed 17 kinds of information needed in order to make recommendations for treatment.

1. Sexual arousal pattern. Is the person sexually aroused by sexual activity between two consenting adults or by nonconsensual sex? Is the person mostly aroused by violence? Is the person sexually attracted to children, and, if so, which sex and what age group?

2. Sexual history. It is often useful to know the extent of previous sexual acting out — but expect denial here — and the extent of appropriate sexual experiences. How many previous offenses has he or she committed against how many victims? What were the ages and sexes of the victims? At what age did the fantasies or offenses begin?

3. Sexual attitudes and knowledge. Many offenders accept beliefs and attitudes that support deviant sexual behavior. Other offenders may have inadequate information about what constitutes "normal" sexual activity.

4. Offense description. Request a detailed account of the circumstances surrounding the offense for which he or she is charged.

5. Chain of thoughts, feelings, and actions leading to offenses. This chain will be discussed at greater length under the heading of relapse prevention. It is important to learn about the thoughts, feelings, and behaviors that preceded the offense. The offender's sexual fantasies should be detailed, as should the plans implemented prior to enacting the crime.

6. Thinking errors. Many sex offenders use distorted thinking styles to justify and rationalize their sexually abusive behavior. These thinking errors contribute to the compulsive nature of many of the resulting crimes.

7. Degree and type of denial. As mentioned previously, denial is a common maneuver used by offenders. Assessing the extent and type of denial, however, is important to treatment planning.

8. Empathy for victims. Many sex offenders do not fully appreciate the impact of their sex offenses on the victims. They may give lip service to their plight, but careful probing often reveals they have little appreciation of the trauma and distress the victims experience. Is the offender merely expressing regret for the victim's experience (sympathy), or is he able to participate in the feelings the victim must have had during and after the experience (empathy)?

9. Degree of antisocial behavior. There are some sex offenders whose deviant sexual behavior is but one of a variety of ways the person acts out in antisocial ways. For example, such a person may rape the woman he finds at a residence he is burglarizing and not feel differently towards her than he does the objects he is stealing.

10. Attitudes toward women. Some sex offenders have hostile feelings toward women and subscribe to many rape myths. Since hostile feelings and rape myths can serve as disinhibitors for sexual acting out, assessing their extent is important.

11. Social skills. Some child molesters have some interest in women but are fearful and anxious around them. This lack of social skills impairs their ability to form satisfying consenting relationships. Other sex offenders are quite socially skilled and use their charm to gain access to children or women. If an offender has no interest in adults, we may not want to increase his social skills because he may only use such knowledge to gain access to children.

12. Assertiveness and aggressiveness. Most sex offenders have in common a lack of appropriate assertiveness. Even sexually assaultive men may in fact alternate between insecurity and aggression and lack of appropriate assertiveness.

13. Marital relationship. Many mental health providers are inclined to emphasize this area of assessment, but its importance to sex-offender treatment, except perhaps in cases of incest, is often not as great as other areas of information already cited. Those providers who focus on strengthening the marital bond seem to assume that the impaired marital relationship caused the sexual acting out by the offender. This cause-and-effect relationship, however, is not established. It could be that pre-existing thoughts, feelings, and behaviors related to sexual offending may be causes of the marital problems.

14. Family problems. This information can be useful, especially in incest cases but, as in the case of marital problems, it is difficult to know which is the cause and which is the effect.

15. Personal/developmental history. This information assesses family of origin issues. Important to this area of assessment is any history of physical or sexual abuse in the offender's childhood.

16. Alcohol use/abuse. Even though alcohol and drugs may release inhibitions against offending, they do not cause sex offenses. In a high percentage of sex offenses, alcohol is present in the offender but reducing alcohol consumption will not by itself eliminate sexual deviancy.

17. Personality traits. Even though personality traits do not explain sexual deviancy, i.e., sexual deviancy may exist without any other form of psychopathology, some personality traits are correlated with abuse. For example, offenders who externalize their problems find it easy to blame their behavior on others.

Depression can lead to sexual acting out as part of a deviant cycle. In addition, depression sometimes develops when the offender is discovered and can lead to suicide.

If the above kinds of information are not readily available from traditional kinds of test batteries, where can useful information be obtained? Specialized sex-offender assessment usually incorporates information from the following sources:

- psychophysiological testing
- clinical interview
- psychological testing
- collateral information

Psychophysiological Testing

Plethysmograph. This instrument electronically measures penile arousal when the offender is presented with audio-visual materials designed to determine sources of his arousal (see Appendix H for a consent form example). It is used only for treatment purposes (as opposed to prosecution or sentencing). Because the presence of arousal to fantasized criminal behavior does not constitute a law violation or indicate that the person has engaged in the deviant behavior, and because some individuals are able to mask their arousal to deviant stimuli, the plethysmograph is not appropriate for criminal prosecution or proving allegations in revocations.

There are two types of plethysmograph gauges currently used. One consists of a light-weight butterfly shaped gauge which fits around the subject's penis. He is seated in a room alone and puts the device on by himself. The other kind of gauge consists of small loop of latex tubing filled with mercury. This strain gauge is then connected to an electronic amplifier similar to one used with the butterfly-shaped gauge. This gauge also fits around the subject's penis.

The central index of change is the penile-erection response, measured by a simple circuit that directly assesses male sexual arousal by monitoring penile tumescence. The sensing device detects the arousal response and sends an electronic signal to a recording device that can read out the minimum, maximum, and all intermediate values of the response (usually in percent of total erection). This is then recorded on a polygraph or moving piece of chart paper on which a pen records changes in penile tumescence.

The erection-response measurement is used to get a profile of the kinds of things that arouse a particular person, the kind of deviant stimuli or nondeviant stimuli that will "turn a person on." Many rapists may have adequate arousal to appropriate descriptions, pictures, videotape sequences of what appear to be people engaging in mutually consenting intercourse. They also may have high arousal to scenes and descriptions of rape or of pure physical assault with no sexual activity involved. The situation may be reversed with pedophiles. These offenders may show no sexual interest in adults, whether male or female, but show extremely high arousal to children. In Figures 3.1 to 3.5 the numbers on the vertical axis represent the percentage of erection which the offender registers. In the first of these figures the arousal pattern of a normal heterosexual person is portrayed. This pattern is also characteristic of many incest offenders.

The person whose arousal pattern is shown in Figure 3.2 shows a very strong attraction to young prepubescent males. He would probably be difficult to treat because of the strength of the deviant arousal and the lack of any attraction to adults of either sex.

The person whose arousal pattern is depicted in Figure 3.3 would be easier to treat than the previous figure, because although he is attracted to adolescent females, he also is attracted to adult women. In this case there is something with which to replace the attraction to children. In the absence of this attraction

Figure 3.1
Normal Plethysmograph Profile

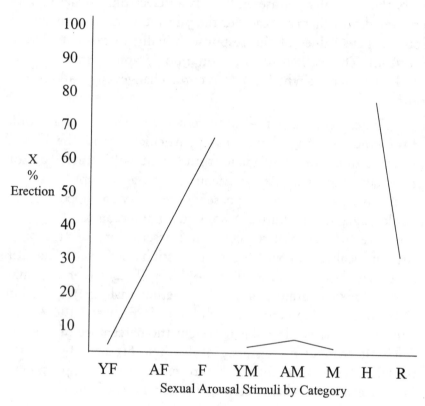

Sexual Arousal Stimuli by Category

Legend:
YF–young female
AF–adolescent female
F–female
YM–young male
AM–adolescent male
M–adult male
H–heterosexual consenting
R–rape

(Source: Quinsey 1990.)

Figure 3.2
Pedophile Plethysmograph Profile

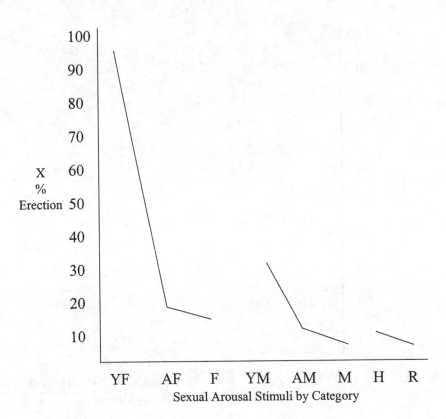

Sexual Arousal Stimuli by Category

Legend:

YF–young female

AF–adolescent female

F–female

YM–young male

AM–adolescent male

M–adult male

H–heterosexual consenting

R–rape

(Source: Bartlow 1974.)

Figure 3.3
Adolescent Female Molester Plethysmograph Profile

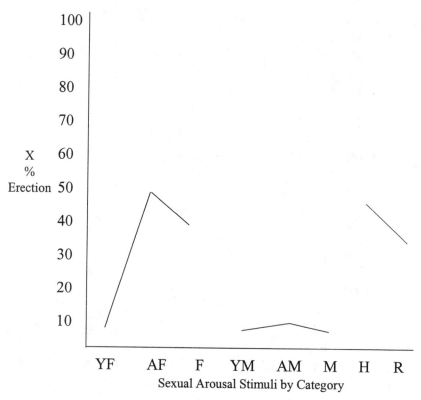

X
%
Erection

Sexual Arousal Stimuli by Category

Legend:

YF–young female
AF–adolescent female
F–female
YM–young male
AM–adolescent male
M–adult male
H–heterosexual consenting
R–rape

(Source: Murphy 1990.)

Figure 3.4
Adolescent Male Molester Plethysmograph Profile

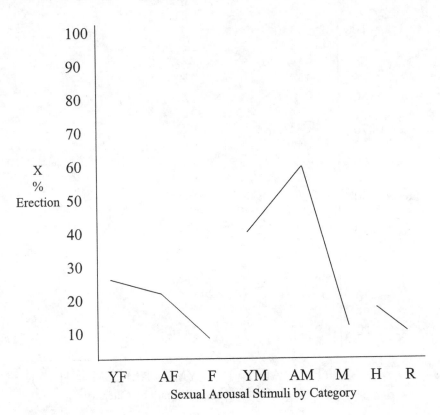

Sexual Arousal Stimuli by Category

Legend:

YF–young female

AF–adolescent female

F–female

YM–young male

AM–adolescent male

M–adult male

H–heterosexual consenting

R–rape

(Source: Stermac 1987.)

Figure 3.5
Polymorphous Perverse Plethysmograph Profile

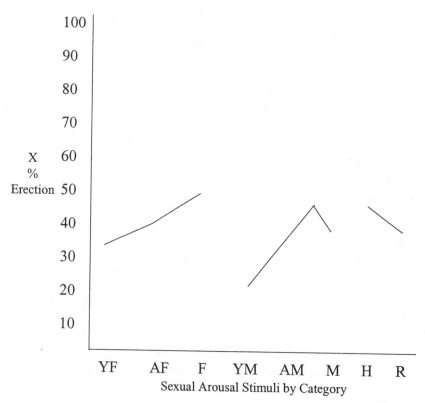

X
%
Erection

Sexual Arousal Stimuli by Category

Legend:

YF–young female

AF–adolescent female

F–female

YM–young male

AM–adolescent male

M–adult male

H–heterosexual consenting

R–rape

(Source: Yochelson 1977.)

to adults, it is difficult with current techniques to generate appropriate sexual interest to agemates.

Molester Plethysmograph Profile

Figure 3.4 depicts the arousal pattern of a pedophile who is attracted to young males but not to adult males or to females of any age.

Figure 3.5 shows the sexual arousal pattern of an offender whose sexual interests are global. He appears to be interested in every category shown.

In fact, the person from whom this record was obtained had molested four of his sisters while growing up. As an adult he molested both his daughters and his sons, both prepubescent and postpubescent. He raped his wife, and in prison he was known as a homosexual rapist!

Plethysmograph Profile

Psychophysiological measurements are crucial to treatment, because self-reports from offenders are not reliable. They tend to deny, rationalize, and minimize everything they have done to make themselves appear as nondeviant as they possibly can. Studies in which sex offenders were first interviewed about the nature and extent of their sexual arousal, who were then subsequently assessed with a plethysmograph, found that in only 30 percent of the cases did the plethysmograph record agree with the offender's self-report. In other words, offenders denied arousal which the plethysmograph documented 70 percent of the time. When these same offenders were then confronted with the psychophysiological data, 70 percent of the deniers (or 49 percent of the total sample) admitted additional arousal. This kind of assessment, then, can be useful in confronting denial.

The self-reports of paraphiliacs are invalid.

Plethysmographic data should only be interpreted by experts in plethysmography. Misinterpretation may be made by those who have inadequate training in the field. The absence of sexual arousal to deviant themes does not necessarily indicate a lack of sexual interest in children. Offender suppression, temporary lack of arousal due to guilt, court sanctions, or other external inhibitors may influence response to testing. Plethysmographic data should be interpreted within the context of a thorough sexual history, review of the offense, and psychological interview with the offender. It is only one tool in the treatment of the sexual offender and may be utilized at the time of evaluation, during treatment to assess the degree to which the client is decreasing his deviant arousal, or as a follow-up to determine if he is maintaining treatment gains. Increases in appropriate arousal will also be indicated in follow-up assessments.

Some sex offenders will try to fake or falsify plethysmographic data. Techniques sometimes used by men being evaluated included masturbating just prior to the recording session, ignoring the slides being presented and fantasizing instead to arousal fantasies, and using aversive imagery. To the trained investigator, however, these ploys are often detectable.

Vaginal probe. The counterpart to the plethysmograph in assessing female sexual arousal is the vaginal probe. This device is potentially useful in assessing female sex offenders' deviant arousal patterns. At the present time, however, it is not widely available or used in conjunction with many sex-offender treatment programs.

Clinical polygraph. The polygraph is an electronic device that measures various reactions of the body to an emotion-elicit-ing stimulus. Polygraph examinations should be ordered by the court as a condition of probation in a majority of sex offender cases. The polygraph is an effective tool for measuring treatment and supervision compliance as well as a deterrent to technical and criminal violations. The polygraph is not viewed by the courts as a violation of personal rights but as an agreement the client has made in accepting probation in lieu of a penitentiary sentence. Because the offender has accepted the probation conditions as a part of probation, a refusal to be polygraphed or "taking the fifth" by the offender should be seen as a potential probation violation and consideration should be given to returning the offender to the sentencing court.

The polygraph examination should be administered by a licensed polygraph examiner and should be ordered at the client's expense. The frequency of examinations may be dictated by the court order and/or at the supervising officer's direction. After the initial assessment, subsequent examinations are administered to determine compliance with the probation conditions as well as progress in treatment, including full disclosure of deviant history and current status of fantasy structure. Periodic polygraphs should be used throughout the probation/parole period, particularly at times when major case issues such as visitation or reunification are being implemented. It may be used prior to the offender's move home, or more commonly three to six months after reunification occurs. The literature regarding sex offenders supports that the polygraph is also an effective tool in conjunction with the penile plethysmograph.

Although psychophysiological assessment instruments are important in overcoming problems associated with offender denial, in monitoring decreases in deviant sexual arousal, and in verifying compliance with treatment and supervision contracts, the unfortunate reality is that this kind of assessment is unavailable. Where it is not feasible to send offenders to clinics in the larger cities where such services are available, the officer needs to be aware that there will be less certainty that the offender's denial is being overcome and therapeutic gains can be verified.

Using psychophysiological measurements in a treatment and supervisory context is controversial and subject to abuse and misinterpretation. The research documents that psychophysiological measurements can be circumvented or defeated by some individuals. This likelihood increases with frequent testing. Furthermore, polygraph results sometimes lead to the conclusion that the person examined was lying when he or she was not. In other instances, people are sometimes believed to have told the truth when in fact they did not. Officers need to be aware these are not infallible instruments, and they should not be relied upon exclusively to assess and monitor sex offenders.

The Interview

It is not uncommon for people to feel uncomfortable about having to interview a sex offender. Dealing with issues such as sexual conduct and denial do not make the interviewing process easy. Offenders often try to control the interview in the way they dress and behave. Attempts to intimidate the interviewer by staring intently at him or her or by getting too close are not unheard of either. Interviewing these kinds of offenders can be easier if the officer uses the principals listed below to guide the interview.

Principles for Interviewing

- **Control the interview**

  Set your own agenda for the interview. Do not let the offender retry the case in the interview. Do not listen to extended explanations of innocence. If a rapist is intimidating to you, leave the office door open and be sure that other people are available nearby. Sit near the door if you feel safer that way. Never see a rapist in any situation in which you do not feel safe. That kind of ambiguity he may use to intimidate you. When you detect nonverbal or verbal attempts to intimidate you, confront them directly. Do not cower or provoke, but do set clear limits on his behavior during the interview.

- **Explain that you are experienced.**

  Let the person know that you have worked with sex offenders before and are familiar with some of the problems presented by these people.

- **Explain that the evaluation will not be confidential.**

  Go over with the offender the purpose of the interview and who will have access to the information. The purpose of the interview is either to assist in completing a presentence investigation or in designing a supervision plan.

- **Describe sex offenders.**

  Many people think that persons who molest children or sexually assault others are morally bankrupt, emotionally depraved individuals who continually fantasize about sexual abuse and constantly search for the next person they might violate. Point out to the person being interviewed that most sex offenders are not like that at all. Some offenders are outstanding teachers, successful bankers, elected officials, attorneys, psychologists, and members of the clergy. For the most part, offenders are decent human being, but who have a major problem when it comes to their sexual behaviors.

- **Describe the dynamics of sex offenses.**

  Discuss the roles that fantasy and planning play in most offenses. If you are interviewing a pedophile, tell the offender that you know about grooming child victims. Say that you know that people are rarely caught for the first offense — that typically the person has offended before and without help will offend again.

- **Describe denial.**

  Let the offender know that most people do attempt to deny the problem and that you have probably heard most ways of denying it. Mention some of the ways offenders deny responsibility for their crimes. You may accidentally hit upon the one the offender had planned to use.

- **Warn of the dangers of making a second mistake.**

  Everyone makes mistakes. The important thing to do is to acknowledge our mistakes. Failing to do this only compounds our difficulties and makes it more likely we will repeat earlier mistakes. It takes a bigger man to admit his mistakes, rather than trying to cover them up.

- **Accept rationalization and minimization.**

  Self-disclosure is an ongoing process, and most offenders do not reveal everything requested in one interview. For the first interview it is sufficient that the offender admit that he or she committed the offenses.

- **Offer empathy when appropriate.**

  It should not be difficult to understand how frightening it would be for a sex offender to tell the truth; how unrealistic society's picture of a sex offender is; what a burden it is to be afflicted with urges most people don't understand or have. But, you should not offer sympathy for the offender's plight as an "innocent" man accused by a lying child of sexual abuse. The important distinction to make here is that between empathy and collusion. Hopefully, it is clear why it is not a good idea to "join" the offender by agreeing how badly he has been treated and how unfair the justice process is. Do not support denial by empathizing. Sometimes, however, it might be appropriate to empathize with minimization by agreeing that it is difficult to be under stress, to have a marriage that isn't working, a wife that doesn't understand or want you. In other words, be prepared to empathize when the offender talks about why he did it but not when he talks about why he did not do it.

- **Explain the necessity of honesty.**

  This is particularly important when you are interviewing the offender after conviction but before sentencing. If he is a candidate for probation and mandated treatment you can explain to him why admitting is in his best interest (e.g., the program will not take denying offenders). If the issue is not whether he will go to prison but for how long, you can make the case that admitting will result in a more favorable report which may affect the length of his sentence. Offenders who deny are showing no interest in working on their problem and should be incarcerated for as long as the law will permit.

- **Do not reduce anxiety.**

  Most offenders experience considerable anxiety after disclosure and sentencing. This a particularly good opportunity for the offender to disclose even more about his offenses. Many interviews, however, are uncomfortable with this level of anxiety (perhaps because of the anxiety it generates in them) and try to put the client at east. This reduction in anxiety may work against disclosure.

- **Use direct victim material.**

  Statements from victims in whatever medium can be helpful in overcoming the offender's denial. Audio and videotaped statements by victims are particularly useful in this regard.

- **Emphasize the burden of secrecy.**

  Most people do not understand how difficult it is to carry around a secret like this. By pointing out this difficulty to the offender you may appeal to the worries that offenders frequently have about what they have done in secret. Emphasize the relief that comes from acknowledging the secret. Most offenders are unable to talk with anyone about their secrets, and keeping these things to oneself takes an enormous amount of energy and vigilance. Being able to finally talk to someone about these secrets offers a tremendous amount of relief.

- **Turn objections against the offenders.**

  If he professes his innocence by virtue of his standing in the community, explain how many sex offenders are just like him — people who function very well except for one area of their lives which is out of control. If they point to their religiosity as a reason they would never do what they have been accused of, point out that all of us make mistakes and religious faith doesn't protect us from doing so.

- **Frame questions in such a way that it becomes easier for the person to admit responsibility.**

  Instead of asking him is he masturbates, ask him how many times a week he masturbates to deviant fantasies. Don't ask him is he planned it but for how long he planned it. Don't ask him whether he had ever done anything like this before, but how many times he had done this before.

- **Confront contradictions.**

  The interviewer can confront the offender with the contradictions in his statements and request an explanation. The most direct approach would be to say, "Your account doesn't make any sense. First you said . . . , but then you said . . . What is the truth in all of this?"

- **Repeat yourself.**

  Sometimes by asking the same question at different point in the interview the offender provides increasing amounts of information. This is particularly true as the offender begins to disclose more as the interview proceeds. If you are questioned about this strategy, tell him that many people remember more as they go along and that you want to give him every opportunity to do the best job he can. A related strategy is to have the offender repeat his accounts more than once.

- **Use successive approximations.**

  If the offender admits something but denies what the victims claims, edge the offender towards disclosure but cutting the difference. Ask him or her about doing something similar. If, for example, he admits fondling but denies penetration, ask him how many times he put his penis against her vagina. If he admits that, come back to the topic later in the interview and ask him how often his penis "slipped a little bit inside."

- **Begin inquiries about sex offenses by asking about the "worst" sex acts.**

  Focus on the most intrusive recollections first, and then go to less threatening experiences. The interviewer should then proceed by going back and forth between the most serious and the less serious acts. Ask the offender to disclose specific information about each victim.

- **Emphasize the "normality" of fantasy and planning.**

  If the offender claims that the incident "just happened," explain that the only person who commits sex offenses without any thought ahead of time is extremely dangerous and perhaps even psychotic. Such persons are nearly impossible to treat and are, therefore, very dangerous. If he didn't know he was going to do it the first time, he could never know when he was going to do it again. Point out that the best disposition for such people is long incarceration.

- **React neutrally to disclosures.**

  Often the interviewer's reactions are quite transparent to the offender. If the interviewer acts surprised, horrified, or gleeful about this success, the offender may retract his statement. The best thing to do is react calmly as though you expected as much.

- **Offer hope.**

Many offenders are discouraged about the prospect for change in their sexual behavior. You can encourage them by talking about people you have known who have had this or a similar problem and who have made progress. Talk about the difference between people who hide from the problem and hope it will go away and the people who have the courage to admit they have a problem and tackle it head on.

Sex Offenders

Sex offense history. Effective treatment begins with a thorough examination of the offender's illegal sexual behavior. The kinds of offenses committed; the number of such offenses; where they occurred; with whom; and the emotional state of the offender just prior to, during, and after each offense. Examples of questions are provided in Chapter 6 under the section on offense history and in Appendix E. The interviewer should have access to police information and victims' statements before beginning this interview.

Sexual history. Another important area to assess prior to treatment implementation is the offender's sexual history (see Appendix F). This history should reflect the offender's past and present sexual behaviors, fantasies, and arousal patterns as well as show the movement from early sexual development to the criminal behavior. Inquiry should be made into how the offender learned about sex; first sexual experience; type and frequency of all types of sexual behavior; experiences with masturbation; sexual fantasy development; specific victims' information such as names, ages, sexes, and relationships to the offender); current methods of sexual expression; degree of satisfaction or frustration in current relationship; current level of understanding or knowledge of human sexuality.

The history should also identify concrete antecedents to the offenses. Knowing about these antecedents leads to a profile of the offender's deviant pattern: high-risk situations, cycles of mood swings or interpersonal conflicts triggering deviant fantasies, use of intoxicants to facilitate and justify loss of sexual control, cognitive distortions such as rationalizations and justifications for the deviant behavior, patterns used to approach and access victims, and masturbatory practices used to reinforce the deviant fantasies and arousal patterns.

Since sexual histories rely on self-report, the accuracy of the information should be tested by requiring a polygraph examination. Offender sexual histories often unfold over time, requiring reassessment of both treatability and risk.

Collateral Information

So far we have discussed information that should be obtained from the offender. Perhaps the most valuable information, however, is what can be gained from other people. The victim's statement to the police and to the child protective services caseworker are important starting points for any evaluation of a sex offender. Statements of family members and acquaintances of the offender and witnesses to the crimes in question are other useful sources of information. In fact, it is probably unwise to conduct an evaluation of a sex offender until the collateral sources of information are available to the officer.

Psychological Tests

A number of specialized testing instruments have been developed to assist in evaluating sex offenders. Probation or parole officers do not need to be personally familiar with the details of each test, but it will help to assess the usefulness of information from mental health professionals to know a little about each of these instruments.

1. *Abel and Becker Cardsort.* Individuals are given cards describing different types of sex acts and asked how arousing or repulsive they find the description. This is also a useful test of

denial. This test can be used with the results of plethysmography and the offender confronted with any discrepancies between the two measures.

2. *Abel and Becker Cognition Scale.* This measures cognitive distortions of child molesters.

3. *Attitudes towards Women Scale.* This measures the subject's opinions of the appropriate roles and rights of women.

4. *Burt Rape-Myth Acceptance Scale.* This measures the degree to which the subject agrees with rape myths, such as "Women who get raped while hitchhiking deserve what they get."

5. *Buss-Durkee Hostility Inventory.* This measures six different subscales of hostility: negativism, resentment, indirect hostility, assault, suspicion, verbal hostility, and irritability.

6. *Family Adaptability and Cohesion Evaluation Scale* (**FACES**). This brief and easy-to-administer test measures family pathology. Cohesion is rated from disengaged to enmeshed and adaptability from rigid to chaotic.

7. *Interpersonal Reactivity Index.* This empathy scale divides empathy into four different components: perspective taking, empathic concern, personal distress, and fantasy scale.

8. *Michigan Alcohol Screening Test* (**MAST**). This measures alcohol abuse.

9. *Multiphasic Sex Inventory.* This is one of the few tests normed on sex offenders. It measures sexual deviancy in *admitting* offenders.

10. *Social Avoidance and Distress Scale* (**SADS**). This test measures the subject's discomfort in social situations and the desire to avoid them.

11. *Wilson Sexual Fantasy Questionnaire.* This measures the extent to which an individual fantasizes about specific types of sexual themes.

Other inventory examples used in evaluating sex offenders are listed below:

12. *Attitudes toward Women*
13. *Clarke Sexual History Questionnaire*
14. *Cognitive Distortions Scale*
15. *Crowne-Marlowe Scale of Social Responsibility*
16. *Sexual Anxiety Inventory*
17. *Situational Competency Test*
18. *Spielberger State-Trait Anger Scale*

4
Sex-Offender Treatment

Behavioral techniques are designed to reduce deviant sexual arousal and to increase appropriate sexual arousal. They cannot be used effectively alone. They will not change the thinking patterns that support sexual deviancy. They will not teach an offender how to avoid high-risk situations. This is because group confrontation and support which are important to a total treatment program will be missing in a purely behavioral treatment program.

Behavioral Treatment

Once an offender has, however, made progress with his thinking errors and has learned to empathize with victims, he can then benefit from appropriate behavioral skills he has learned. He knows he now has the tools to reduce his deviant arousal. Thus there is a need to consider boredom tapes, covert sensitization, aversive conditioning, and other behavioral techniques.

Boredom Tapes*

While it may be difficult to get sex offenders to comply, boredom tapes are a powerful technique. These tapes are just too aversive for many offenders. Only those who are genuinely interested in getting better and willing to put the time and energy into it will be able to benefit from these tapes.

Boredom tapes are a way of wearing the offender out of a deviant sexual attraction. The offender is asked to masturbate alone while talking into a tape recorder. He first masturbates to a nondeviant sexual fantasy until orgasm or until a set amount of time has elapsed if he cannot achieve orgasm. He then masturbates to a deviant fantasy for the remainder of an hour, usually 50 to 55 minutes. Although the technique is deceptively simple, there are ways to subvert it so that it either is ineffective or actually increases deviant arousal. For this reason it requires close monitoring.

Once the offender understands the procedure, he is instructed to write out a consenting, nondeviant sexual fantasy for homework. Then he is asked to write out his offense, paying special attention to the parts of the offense he has been using for masturbation. This description is then broken into discrete parts and each part rated in terms of its arousal value. The first tape is then made to the most arousing part of the deviant fantasy. The most arousing part of the fantasy is repeated over and over until the offender no longer finds it arousing.

Programs differ on how many tapes should be produced. The minimum seems to be around 20 tapes spread over five weeks but can be three or four times that amount. The best rule is probably to consider discontinuing when the arousal appears to be completely satiated as determined by a plethysmograph. Offenders need to be carefully monitored to detect conscious faking or moving on too soon to a more exciting part of the fantasy.

---

*For a review of treatment tapes see Salter 1989.

A variation of this technique is verbal satiation (Knopp 1984). This intervention involves a simple procedure used three times a week. The person is hooked into the plethysmograph while wearing a headset. He is asked to sit there and recite deviant sexual fantasies aloud for 30 minutes without stopping. His headset is hooked up to a voice-operated relay; if he pauses for more than five seconds, a loud tone goes off in his ears and the only way he can shut the tone off is to start speaking again. The deviant fantasy is monitored by staff. Within two or three weeks the person usually has totally exhausted his repertoire of effective fantasies. If he cannot think of anything to say, the tone goes off in his ears, so he has to talk, and only deviant fantasies will do. It becomes boring.

There are a number of problems with boredom tapes. Some offenders deny any sexual fantasies when they masturbate. In some cases this is just a part of the denial system. In other instances the offender may truly not use deviant sexual fantasies. Other offenders may exhibit a high sex drive which causes them to ejaculate not only to the nondeviant fantasy but to the subsequent deviant ones as well.

In some cases offenders will resist the procedure on religious grounds. Here again the resistance may be an attempt to avoid treatment (most probably masturbated prior to public discovery). The difficulty is that judges, clergy, and others in the community may support the offender's scruples on this issue and inadvertently collude with him.

If the technique is successful in lowering the offender's sexual interest, the lowered sex drive may be replaced by anxiety or depression. In many cases the deviant sexual interest was a major component of the offender's life. If he was molesting to distract himself from other problems, he may find he still has the anxiety from other problems. In any case, depression is common for sex offenders in treatment, and suicide is a significant risk.

For reasons not detectable, sometimes boredom tapes simply do not work. Failures are sometimes reported with older pedophiles with no interest in adult sex and many decades of sexual interest in children.

Some offenders report a return to a deviant interest in as little as six weeks following the cessation of behavioral treatment. At the other extreme, some offenders have reported no rebound after a year or more.

Covert Sensitization

A second technique for reducing deviant arousal is covert sensitization (see Wolf in Salter 1989). This technique involves pairing the deviant fantasy with an aversive fantasy and/or an interruption fantasy followed by an escape scene. The procedure begins by explaining to the offender that he has increased his sexual attraction to children, for instance, by pairing it with something pleasurable, such as sexual arousal or orgasm. The strategy of this technique is to reverse the process by pairing the deviant sexual fantasy with something aversive.

The deviant fantasy should not just be a straight sexual fantasy with a child or of violent sex with an adult, but should include the offense chain as developed in his work with relapse prevention (discussed later in this chapter). The part of the offense chain chosen should be the part that definitely moves toward the molestation or assault. It should not be so close to the offense that in real life he would find it difficult to exit because of the impulse strength at the time (see Figure 4.1).

The deviant fantasy should last anywhere from 30 seconds to one minute or at most two. It should stop at the urge to commit the offense — before any aspects of the actual molestation take place.

The aversive scene must be developed with the offender. Asthma attacks, near-drownings, and other personal experiences

Figure 4.1
An Illustration of Deviant Fantasy

You are restless. It is about three o'clock in the morning and you cannot sleep. You tell yourself you are going to go to the bathroom. You get up, you go to the bathroom, you urinate, and you continue to stand there. You are thinking, "Little Sally is sleeping in the room next door." You tell yourself, "Maybe I'd better check on her just to see if she kicked her covers off or something." As you are thinking that, you kind of put your hand down on your penis and you feel your excitement. You tell yourself, "She is sound asleep — she won't know if I was in there or not." You go up to her door, telling yourself she is sound asleep and you are just going to check on her, feeling sexual excitement, thinking about touching her, thinking you will just slip up her nightgown a little bit and maybe just look at her, and getting more excited. You are thinking about doing that, with your hand on the door knob, getting really excited now, really turned on, and you gently, carefully, being really quiet, open that door, you open that door thinking about touching her . . . and you suddenly realize there is something on the floor. There is something moving on the floor in the bedroom. My God, my God, you say it is a snake! There is more than one. There are creepy, crawly snakes all over and you can see their little forked tongues, see their beady eyes. They are moving toward you. You are just terrified standing there; you want to run, but you are just scared. A cold chill runs up and down your body. Your body gets tight. They are moving toward you. God, these cold slimy snakes are moving toward you. One of them is on your toe now.

Source: Wolfe 1989.

may be used as well as the adverse social consequences of getting caught. This part of the fantasy should be longer than the first part.

Sometimes escape scenes are added to the end of the fantasy. The escape scene can be an appropriate interaction with an adult. "I didn't go into my daughter's room. I get back in bed with my wife. I reach over to touch her. I slip my . . . ." It can also be a scene of the positive consequences of being in control. "I haven't molested any children. I'm not afraid so much any more. I don't have those dreams of prison. I'm enjoying life more this way. It's a relief."

The cycle of deviant fantasy followed by aversive consequences (and sometimes an escape scene) should be repeated to make a session totaling approximately 15 minutes. To break up the trials a neutral scene can be constructed between the aversive scene (or even the escape scene) and the beginning of the deviant fantasy.

These tapes are briefer and less aversive than boredom tapes. Typically, there are fewer of them. Consequently, offenders are more willing to institute them again if their deviant arousal returns at another time.

Problems associated with this technique include scenes that are not vivid for the offender and habituation to the aversive scenes so that they are no longer frightening.

Aversive Conditioning*

Aversive conditioning or assisted covert conditioning is the third behavioral technique used in specialized sex-offender treatment programs. This involves exposing the offender to an arousing stimulus, usually either a slide of a young child or an audiotape of a violent sexual attack and pairing this with an aversive smell (olfactory aversion). The slides typically will be of chil-

*Adapted from Salter 1989.

dren of similar age and sex to those the offender is attracted to.
The most sophisticated version involves having the offender attached to the plethysmograph while viewing the slide. When the
machine registers sexual arousal, it automatically releases an offensive odor. Less sophisticated approaches involve the offender's
self-report with a self-administered aversive smell. The offender
begins describing a deviant sexual fantasy and when he reports
arousal, takes the top off of a plastic film canister filled with ammonia and inhales. The smell stops the sexual arousal and cognitively pairs the previously arousing stimulus with an aversive
smell. The advantage of this technique is that it is portable, can
accompany the offender, and used unobtrusively in public whenever he finds himself sexually aroused by a child or some deviant
fantasy.

Orgasmic Reconditioning*

Most treatment efforts for sex offenders have been devoted
to the development of intervention strategies to reduce inappropriate sexual arousal. There is comparatively little recent work
concerning methods to increase nondeviant sexual arousal. It has
been shown that simple exposure to an explicit heterosexual film
may facilitate the development of appropriate heterosexual
arousal (Bartlow 1974). The gradual superimposition of an appropriate consensual, heterosexual stimulus on an inappropriate or
deviant one, while gradually fading out the deviant cue, appears
to result in increases in nondeviant arousal. However, increasing
nondeviant sexual arousal does not guarantee decreases in deviant
sexual arousal.

In keeping with a conditioning model of sexual behavior, attempts have been made to "recondition" sexual preferences by
pairing the reinforcing effects of genital stimulation and orgasm
with sexual fantasies involving sex between two consenting
adults. The offender in this case is asked to become aroused and

---

*Adapted from Quinsey and Earls 1990.

masturbate to a deviant sexual fantasy. At the moment of ejaculatory inevitability, the deviant fantasy is switched to an appropriate theme; and gradually, throughout therapy, the moment of switching fantasies is moved backward in time until the offender is able to masturbate and achieve orgasm using the appropriate sexual fantasy.

Although the behavioral techniques discussed above have sometimes been useful in eliminating or modifying a sex offender's deviant sexual arousal, by themselves they do not significantly reduce the chances of reoffending. Some sex offenders whose deviant sexual arousal has been extinguished may experience spontaneous recovery at some later date. This is why other contributing factors to the person's offense pattern must be addressed in treatment.

Cognitive Restructuring*

In general there are three approaches used to describe the role of sexual-abuse cognitions, such as thoughts, attitudes, ideas, and memories (Stermac and Segel 1987). Cognitive behavioral distortions refer to self-statements made by offenders that allow them to deny, minimize, justify, and rationalize their behavior. In one approach these cognitive factors are not seen as direct causes of deviant sexual behavior, but as steps offenders take to justify and thus maintain their behavior. "It was sex education," or "I was only playing," are examples of cognitive distortions.

A second approach to cognitive factors is derived from a more feminist perspective toward rape which describes attitudes supportive of rape, such as rape myth acceptance, sex-role stereotyping, adversarial sexual beliefs, and acceptance of interpersonal violence against women. Certain beliefs — such as sex must be coerced from a woman, men have the right to request sex from a woman, if women were more protected and sheltered they would be less vulnerable to rape, and women who are assaulted are

---

*Adapted from Murphy 1990.

somehow partly to blame — serve to disinhibit the behavior of some men and make it more likely to act on assaultive impulses under certain circumstances. Evidence implies these kinds of beliefs have causal significance and may be a factor contributing to sexual aggression.

The third approach to cognitive factors is drawn from the criminological literature epitomized by Yochelson and Samenow's (1977) description of thinking errors. This model proposes a number of lifelong patterns of distorted thinking by individuals who engage in criminal behavior. It proposes that such errors of thinking tend to be pervasive in the offender's life and not limited to sex offending.

It should be apparent that restructuring must address the mistaken beliefs held by sex offenders for whom a change in behavior is sought. Knopp (1984) listed the following seven thinking errors — while not shared by all — are held by many sex offenders:

Seven Mistaken Beliefs of Sex Offenders

1. **Love, Approval, and Respect.** The belief that it is an absolute necessity to have love, approval, and respect from peers, family, and friends. The problem with this belief is that it is impossible to please all the people in your life.

   Criminal Pride. This occurs when the offender believes he is better than other people even when this is clearly not so. To the criminal, being at the same level as others is a put down, a blow to his self-image. A criminal's pride will let him do anything to save face.

   Sentimentality. Criminals are often excessively sentimental toward their mothers, old people, invalids, animals, babies, and their plans for the future. The criminal will often use his soft sentimental side to build up an image of himself as a good, caring person, and to justify the hurtful and criminal things he does which often hurt the people he cares for most.

2. **Perfectionism.** The belief that you must be unfailingly competent and almost perfect in all you do. The results of this belief are self-blame for certain failure, lowered self-image, perfectionistic standards applied to mate and friends and fear of attempting to do things.

   Zero State. This is defined as the periodic experience of oneself as being nothing, "a zero," a feeling of absolute worthlessness, hopelessness, and futility. Basically, the offender sees everything in extremes, either better or worse than it really is, all or nothing.

   "I Can't." This is what the criminal says to express his refusal to act responsibly. For the offender, the excuse "I can't" is an easy way out, a way to avoid responsibilities even though at the time, the criminal believes he can do anything he wants to and there's nothing he can't do.

3. **Awfulizing.** This is the belief that it is horrible when people and things are not the way you would like them to be. To the criminal it is awful if he can't be the "big shot" he thinks he is. Anything that doesn't go the criminal's way is awful and he deals with it by acting out criminally.

   Power and Control. The offender needs power and control over others. His greatest power and excitement is doing the forbidden and getting away with it. Generally, the occasions when the criminal appears to show an interest in a responsible activity are usually opportunities for him or her to exercise power and control. Some power and control tactics are deceiving, domineering, intimidating, and manipulating.

   Ownership. This is an extremely high form of control of events and situations. When an offender wants something, it is as good as his. "Belonging" is established in his mind and he feels perfectly justified in getting his way. Anyone who does not agree with the offender's beliefs, expectations, or demands is seen as a threat, as though that person were taking away something that actually belonged to the offender.

4. **Externalizing Blame.** This is the belief that external events cause human misery, and that you must control the external events in order to create happiness or avoid sorrow. The criminal believes that other people and situations cause the moods he is in. He does not accept responsibility for the situation he is in.

   Victim Stance. This occurs when the offender is held accountable for his own irresponsible actions, and then blames others and pictures himself as the victim. When the criminal is in a victim stance, he is usually in a state of self-pity; and he does not want to own up to the fact that many of the things that went wrong were either his own doing or were made worse by his own irresponsible actions.

5. **Avoidance.** This is the belief that it is easier to avoid life's difficulties, responsibilities, and problems than it is to face up to them. For the offender avoidance is the easy way out of something that he is obligated to do but does not want to do. Some of the things the offender avoids are keeping appointments, going to work, keeping promises, paying bills, spending time with family, supporting and disciplining children, and being faithful to his spouse.

   Closed Channel. This is one of the key tactics the offender uses to resist change and avoid treatment. The offender is often secretive, has a closed mind, and is self-righteous.

   Failure to Make an Effort or Endure Adversity. Effort here refers to doing things that you do not want to do. The offender refuses to endure the adversity of responsible living. The main adversity for the offender is failure to control; failure to be a big shot.

6. **Lack of Empathy.** This occurs frequently when the offender sees people as objects. He has no concern or compassion for people's needs or feelings. He doesn't care for anyone except himself and his own well-being. He does what he has to do for his own survival no matter who he hurts in the process.

    Uniqueness. The offender emphasizes his total difference from other people. He feels himself to be special, "one of a kind." He demands special treatment and consideration from others without understanding that others have needs, want, and desires just as he does.

    Failure to Meet Obligations. The offender cannot keep his word, especially if what he says he will do interferes with what he wants to do. He lets a lot of people down because he cannot commit himself to keeping his promises, spending time with family, paying bills, supporting his family, or even holding down a job.

7. **Lack of Time Perspective.** This is a mistaken belief in the sense that an offender has no concept of the length of life or a lifetime. The past and the future are not considered before he acts out criminally.

    Instancy. This occurs when the offender is unwilling to wait or work for what he wants. He gets upset and angry when others do not instantly meet his demands. "I want what I want and I want it now!"

    Superoptimism. The offender will not get caught this time as he cuts off his fear and forgets that this behavior was a mistake in the past. The offender's mind works in such a way that a chance or possibility for something (like a job for example) is as good as his. When acting out criminally the offender mistakenly believes "There's no way I'll get caught."

The three cognitive restructuring models developed in different contexts yet they share many things in common. They all deal with the way individuals perceive (or misperceive) and attend to environmental cues, as well as the way they process information and the way each person evaluates or misevaluates the consequences of the behavior. Bandura's (1977) social learning theory provides a model that incorporates aspects of a number of all three of these approaches. He describes three major cognitive processes, and a number of subcategories within each of them that allow individuals to basically disengage the normal self-evaluative thoughts that tend to influence human behavior. This model is a means of summarizing the cognitive processes hypothesized to be relevant to sex offenders. Moreover, it may serve to place the self-statements heard from sex offenders within a conceptual framework (see Table 4.1).

Changing Cognitions

A number of approaches have been used to change cognitions. The following standard procedures used to change any kind of cognition have been adapted for use with sex offenders.

Provide the offender with a rationale for the role distortions play in sex offenses and the need to change them. The following justification example might be given to an offender:

Since sex offenders have feelings toward other people, and at some level they know they are hurting someone else, they have to do something to avoid these uncomfortable feelings. They may tell themselves that what they are doing is not bad, or the child (adult) really wanted to do this, or it could have been worse. Different offenders tell themselves different things. After a while, the things you say to yourself become almost automatic and you may not even realize you are saying them. Our job is to help you identify these things and try to show you why many of them are not true. We call these things you say to yourself excuses, justifications, minimizations, and cognitive distortions. I want to

Table 4.1
A Social Learning Model of Cognitive Factors in Sex Offenders

General category and specific process	Specific sex offender statements
Justifying reprehensible conduct	
• Moral justification	"It was sex education."
• Psychological justification	"My offense occurred as a result of my wife's lack of understanding, my drinking, my drug abuse."
• Palliative comparisons	"But I never had intercourse with the child."
• Euphemistic labeling	"I was only fooling around." "I was only playing."
Misperceiving consequences	
• Minimizing consequences	"The child didn't suffer."
• Ignoring the consequences	"I don't care."
• Misattributing the consequence	"If the parents (or agency officials involved in the case) had been more sensitive, the victim wouldn't have so many problems."
Devaluing and attributing blame to the victim	
• Dehumanization	"She was a whore anyway."
• Attribution of blame	"Most women want to be raped."

Source: Murchy 1990.

warn you that this part of the treatment is not going to be comfortable. The more we help you identify the excuses you have been making and help you realize that they aren't true, the more you are going to have to face that you've potentially caused harm. We also feel that because you are here you really want to do something about your behavior even though it hurts (Murphy 1990).

Offenders need accurate information about sexual abuse and the impact of such abuse on victims. To accomplish this a number of educational materials such as books and movies are introduced, presented from a victim's standpoint, or planned interactions with victim advocates, victim counselors, or victims themselves are arranged. Offenders need to learn about the long-term consequences of abuse on victims. They may be asked to develop a written list of the impact sexual abuse has had on their victims and the impact abuse could potentially have on other victims.

Help offenders recognize their distortions and assist them in developing strategies to counter them. This is typically done in groups, where each offender receives feedback from the therapist and other group members about the inaccuracy of his cognitions. For example, consider an incest offender who has molested his 10-year-old daughter. He might agree with the statement, "If my daughter had said no, I would have stopped." This statement contains a number of distortions including that a child can consent to have sex with an adult; that if a child does not say no, they have agreed to the sexual act; and that it is the child's responsibility to stop sexual abuse. After an offender has made such a statement, he can be questioned about whether he would allow his 10-year-old daughter to buy toys (clothes, etc.) on credit. Few offenders would allow this. When asked to explain why he is apt to say that the child would be too young to enter such a legal contract and would not understand the consequences of entering such a contract. At that point the offender can then be con-

fronted with the proposition that children are too young to nego-
tiate a sexual contract with an adult, since they are also too immature and lack sufficient knowledge to understand the
consequences of such an involvement.

When the offender is asked what happens when his 10-year-
old daughter says no when she is asked to clean her room, he usually responds by saying that the child would be punished in some
way. Then it is pointed out that children are punished almost
every time they say no to adults, especially adults who are
authority figures. Therefore, it would be extremely hard for a
child to say no to her father regarding sexual activity when the
child is punished for saying no at other times.

Role playing in a group format can be used to get offenders
to challenge the distortions. The therapist may role play the molester who uses various distortions, while an actual offender is
asked to play the probation officer or police officer.

Another approach that is useful in helping offenders identify and confront distortions is to have the person and therapist
review the verbal and masturbatory satiation tapes, with the focus on recognizing distortions. These tapes involve detailed fantasies and include perceived victim reactions, often a rich source of
information regarding the offender's distortions. The tape would
be stopped at each point where a distortion is discovered. Attempts are made to point out to the offender why the distortion
is false, then to challenge and confront him in order to generate
alternative and more appropriate statements. They may be asked
to keep a list of distortions as they are identified. They may also
be asked to write out reasons why the distortions are false.

Sex-Offender Groups*

Sex-offender groups should include eight to 16 people and
meet at least once a week for an hour and a half. The time spent

---

*Adapted from Salter 1989.

in treatment should usually be between 18 and 30 months. In addition to group treatment, individual treatment is often recommended for sex offenders. **Individual treatment used by itself in treating sex offenders is unlikely to be as effective as group treatment, because of the propensity of these clients to be manipulative and to deny responsibility.**

Tardiness and absence from group sessions should be confronted. Few excuses should be accepted. As a last resort, missing group meetings should lead to revocation hearings. The reason for such harsh consequences for missing group meetings is the recognition that minor infractions tend to precede major ones.

Groups should be heterogeneous. Child molesters will not see their own thinking errors but can see the thinking errors of rapists. Likewise, rapists can see that child molesters are not just "loving children."

Some groups operate with a peer leader who is elected each week. Two persons are nominated each week, and before the election each person nominated is required to say what he or she would do if elected. The voting must be unanimous. Opting for peer-led groups prevents power struggles from developing between therapists and group members. Offenders often act in collusion with one another to defeat the therapist. Little responsible work is accomplished this way. Consequently, in peer-led groups the leader's job is to keep the groups task-oriented and to confront backsliding members. If he or she fails to do this, the therapist will confront the peer leader.

Candidates for the group must achieve membership status. In order to become members they must:

- learn the group rules and norms
- admit offense responsibility
- talk about previous offenses and/or other deviant sexual interests

- describe deviant masturbation fantasies
- be helpful to other group members
- complete homework assignments
- follow rules of program
- ask each member to accept the candidate as a member into the group

Some groups incorporate an opening ritual in every meeting (Pithers 1991). Each member states his victim's first name, what he did to her or him, his relapse risk factors (see discussion about relapse prevention below), risk situations he has encountered during the past week, and any lapses he has had in the past week. The membership procedures and opening rituals are a way to increase the value of the group to each offender.

Following the opening ritual, the members are asked if anyone wants to talk about a personal problem. Once that is done, homework assignments from the previous meeting are discussed. In some groups satiation tapes are played and discussed.

Over time the group may address a variety of relevant topics such as victim empathy (see discussion below), personal victimization, social skills, anger management, conflict resolution, and interpersonal and communication skills.

Some of the things to look for in group meetings include the following:

Total denial. The offender should be told that the group is only for offenders who have a problem. If he doesn't have a problem, he should tell it to the judge. The group's time will not be wasted by attempts to retry his case.

Minimizing. If other offenders don't jump on someone who is minimizing, hold them accountable. If they can't see it in others, they will not be able to see it in themselves.

Externalizing. Offenders will try to blame others for their problems. For example, it's their wife's fault, their child's fault, the stress at work, or financial stress. Here again, other offenders should be alert to this tactic and confront it.

Use of language. If an offender says that he and the five-year-old girl "made love," he is still not taking responsibility for the abuse. Confront it.

Doing nothing. This refers to the offender who has no agenda items, with no deviant thoughts or fantasies the preceding week. He reports no lapses. He says nothing that could be interpreted as entering his deviant cycle. He says little in the group to avoid being a focus of group attention. This type of member should be confronted on doing nothing in the group. Having no deviant thoughts, feelings, or fantasies in a sex offender group is not a sign of progress; it is a sign of covering up.

Premature termination. This refers to the offender (often the "do-nothing" person described above) who is sure he will never offend again and does not need to be in the group. He has put all of the problems that led to his crime behind him. During his time in the group he may have demonstrated little struggle with his problems. Having tried a "flight into health," he is ready to run from treatment altogether.

Deviant arousal. Sometimes offenders admit to masturbating to deviant fantasies or seeking a "target" and allowing deviant thoughts to enter their heads. They cannot be directly confronted about this because they will simply withhold the information next time. Instead, they should be praised for being honest about their temptations, but given assignments to reduce the deviant arousal. Boredom tapes or covert sensitization tapes may be used (discussed earlier in this chapter).

Entering deviant cycle. Indications that an offender is entering a deviant cycle include:

- "Victim stancing." The offender portrays himself as the victim, for example, by saying, "I loved her and would have done anything for her. This is the thanks I get," or

"By taking my child away from me, you have undermined my role as a father to the child."

- A cruising rapist who left the house after a fight with his wife to drive around and "cool off."

- An offender who has begun to think that the neighbor boy has a large yard to rake and might enjoy a Coke to refresh himself.

Using religion. It is not uncommon for sex offenders to "discover" religion after being apprehended as a way of avoiding treatment. They believe they no longer have to worry about offending again, because they have turned this problem over to the Lord. They object to boredom tapes because masturbation is against their religion. They can be told they may certainly use their faith to help them get through treatment and resist temptation, but they will not be allowed to use religion to avoid treatment.

If an offender is noncompliant, for instance does not attend group regularly, does not complete homework assignments, does not participate in opening ritual, does not participate in group, and resists encouragement to identify risk factors to his reoffending, he can be placed on treatment probation. A document should be drawn up that specifically addresses the treatment-provider complaints. The offender is then given a set period of time to correct his behavior. If he does not improve, he can be dropped from the group and referred back to the supervising officer. The supporting document would also be sent to the officer and could be introduced into any subsequent legal proceeding with the offender.

Medication

The use of treating sex offenders with anti-androgens — medications which reduce the levels of male hormones in the body — has considerable appeal for many segments of the public, but its use is controversial. Clinical reports on the use of antihormone therapy have shown mixed outcomes, and side effects from the medications are reported as problematic. The philosophy underlying this approach to treating sex offenders is that some sex offenses reflect intense antisocial drives potentially treatable with medication. When this kind of treatment is used by itself, the changes, such as reduction in the strength of arousal), produced by the medication are temporary. Sexual arousal to inappropriate stimuli is reported to return when the offender is taken off of the drug. Antihormone treatment takes immediate effect. It is easily administered and monitored, and it is relatively inexpensive.

Advocates of this treatment approach argue that it restrains sexual criminality while at the same time allowing for a fairly normal sex life. Weekly injections of the drug provide the potential for compulsive offenders to curb their sexual drive and sexual fantasies through suppression of the production of the male hormone testosterone. Reducing testosterone levels is thought to increase the offender's capacity for self-control and to diminish obsessive ruminations and preoccupations that they are unable to exclude from their minds (Berlin 1982). The most compulsive paraphiliacs, namely, exhibitionists, and male pedophiles attracted to the same sex, along with voyeurs, and masochists are most frequently targeted for this kind of treatment. It is less often recommended for compulsive rapists. The injections do not produce impotence but have the effect of "cooling down" the sex offender while other psychotherapeutic and behavioral interventions can be administered. In some cases the injections may be lowered in dosage and maintained for an extended period of time.

Depo-provera is probably the most commonly used medication for treatment in this country. Injected into the muscles on a weekly basis at a dose of around 500 mg, it reduces testosterone production and returns the levels of this hormone to pre-pubertal male levels. Effective rehabilitation in the treatment of sex offenders with depo-provera is dependent upon careful selection of appropriate candidates. Only offenders who qualify for the diagnosis of paraphilia, characterized by recurrent, persistent fantasies about deviant sex and erotic cravings, are good candidates for this kind of treatment. Depo-provera does not treat aggression per se, but it may reduce sex-related aggression (Berlin and Meinecke 1981).

Many researchers employing drug treatments remain enthusiastic about their potential, and there is the belief that new and more sophisticated drugs such as cyproterone hold promise for reducing deviant arousal while leaving normal arousal intact. A middle-of-the-road position might be that, at the present time, drug treatment should be considered for a small minority of offenders for whom other treatments have consistently failed or are unsuitable.

The medical approach to sex-offender treatment is another instance of limited availability. For the most part, this kind of treatment will only be found in the larger metropolitan areas. Where it may be impractical to expect an offender to travel to such a facility, disposition options will be more limited. In remote areas of the state some of the offenders who might be good candidates for pharmacological treatment may have to be incarcerated in order to insure the safety of the community.

The use of depo-provera, as indicated above, is controversial. Questions raised by Lockhart and associates (1988) include:

1. **Its short-term negative effects.** These include weight gain, hypertension, high blood pressure, hot flashes, cold sweats, nightmares, mild elevation of blood sugar in some clients, weakness and fatigue, loss of some body hair, and tenderness in the testes because it slows or shuts off their functioning.

2. **Its potential for more harmful long-range effects.** It is difficult to pinpoint the long-range effects of this medication because the longest period of time humans have been receiv-

ing injections is 12 to 17 years. There is some concern that the drug may be carcinogenic (cancer producing). The Food and Drug Administration has approved the drug for treating inoperable cancer of the endometrium and kidneys, but not specifically for the treatment of sex offenders.

3. **Its potential for use under conditions that are involuntary, unmonitored, and indiscriminately punitive rather than remedial.** Most experts are opposed to the use of the drug as punishment. Responsible practitioners administer the drug only under conditions considered voluntary (see the consent form example in Appendix J). Some uninformed judges, however, erroneously view depo-provera as a panacea and have meted out sentences *requiring* the offender to receive such injections. When this happens the drug is being called upon as a punitive alternative to incarceration.

4. **Its effectiveness in controlling sexually aggressive behaviors.** Some treatment programs report encouraging results using medication, for example, the Johns Hopkins' program. Other accounts call into question its efficacy in reducing deviant sexual fantasies and deviant arousal. It may be these disparities in results reflect the different criteria used to determine eligibility for drug treatment.

Other medications have occasionally been used to counter the obsessive-compulsive nature of their deviant fantasies. The outcome data on these medications is anecdotal at this point. Two of the medications used have been Anafranil and Prozac (both are anti-depressant medications).

Re-education and Resocialization

The re-education and resocialization agendas in sex-offender treatment programs are implemented through a wide array of restorative interventions that can be called upon to meet the offender's particular needs and deficits. Many treatment programs consist solely of psycho-educational modules that address primarily nonsexual issues such as social competence. Increasing assertiveness, social competence, and sex education without addressing the offending behavior, the motivating sexual desire, and the supporting cognitive distortions can be dangerous. Such "treated" offenders would simply be more skilled at accessing victims.

Gender-Role Behavior

Many sex offenders seem to have bought into the "masculine mystique" of our culture that says men are strong and powerful, must not be expressive, and should get whatever they want. In comparing themselves to that image, not surprisingly, they find that they fall far short. Consequently, a lot of their energies are directed toward somehow trying to live up to this image they have in their heads of how a man should be. It could be that the real issue for sex offenders is often not how they relate to women, but how they feel about themselves compared to other men. Any difficulties relating to women, then, may be a result of their own failing self-image rather than a lack of social skills.

Not only do many sex offenders view women as filling subservient roles, they rarely experience positive, nurturing relationships with men. Instead, their experience all too often with men is that of abandonment, abuse, and fear. Perhaps for this reason offenders tend to over-invest in women. Because they have not developed much range in emotional expression, they put a great deal of emphasis on sexuality as an expression of acceptance and approval. To be rejected by a woman is to be devastated because it underscores their abandonment and isolation and leaves them with few alternatives for any sense of ego enhancement or personal worth (Groth 1983).

Discussion groups focus on gender issues, address macho behavior, and examine attitudes toward the role of women and men in society with an emphasis on redefining traditional roles. Female volunteers can bring a woman's point of view to such discussions and counter male/female role stereotyping.

Sexuality

Most treatment programs include a unit on correcting the lack of knowledge about human sexuality. Many offenders are ashamed of their own sexuality. The whole topic of sex is viewed in a negative light. "You don't have sex with anyone you respect except to have children." There is often a dichotomy apparent in discussions about women by sex offenders. There are the "good" women on the pedestal and the "other" women who are the ones to have fun with. These latter women are "bad," so what is done to them does not really matter. Their own negative feelings about sex are attributed to women who are often described as being seductive and, by implication, "bad."

Sex from the sex-offender's standpoint is often seen as something degrading or dirty. If sex is degrading, then it can be used to degrade a person. In this way, sex becomes the means of expressing nonsexual needs.

The more effective sex-offender treatment programs encourage positive and appropriate sexuality. Issues such as sexual dysfunction are addressed, as are desensitizing sexual phobias, learning sexual communication skills, examining sexual behavior and values, and both viewing and discussing sexually explicit audio-visual materials.

Personal Victimization and Trauma

Many sex offenders were victims of childhood sexual assault or molestation. The average age at the time of that victimization is about nine years old. The percentage of offenders who have been victimized in this way varies from one study to another. The rates vary from a low of 20 percent to a high of almost 100 percent. Victimization rates may be higher for pedophiles, than for rapists and, in the former case, the perpetrator is more likely to be a person outside the family than is true in the case of the rapist (Seghorn et al. 1983).

Early psychological trauma of this kind usually generates severe emotional distress and decreases stress tolerance for a number of reasons. First, it provides a dramatic demonstration of human frailty. These events lead many people to see the world around them as a particularly threatening, hostile, and dangerous place. Second, childhood trauma may sometimes disrupt the normal developmental processes leading to emotional maturity. That is, the important process of acquiring adequate coping skills may be sabotaged, yielding a psychologically crippled adult. Third, these traumatic events may leave the person with specific emotional wounds that are easily reopened by stressful events during adulthood.

> " . . . when the victimization goes unrecognized and goes unaddressed with no intervention, perhaps, for the male, one way of moving from being the helpless victim is to become the more powerful victimizer" (Groth 1983).

Treatment programs use a variety of victim counseling skills to help the offender work through the problems associated with his or her own sexual abuse. All programs, while helping the offender deal with his own victimization, insist that he take responsibility for the offense and realize these early experiences cannot be "blamed" for his own unacceptable conduct as an adult.

Empathy

Most sex offenders feel little concern for their victims. They usually fail to appreciate how their abusive actions as perpetrators have impacted their victims. To help the offender understand the plight of his victims, group therapy, individual counseling, role plays, and feedback from victims of sexual assault are used. This component of a sex-offender treatment program probably should be introduced fairly early in the treatment process, since it may increase an offender's willingness to take responsibility for his actions and actively participate in programs designed to prevent his reoffending.

The victim-empathy process can effectively be addressed in group therapy (Pithers 1991). The first stage consists of having group members read several books written by victims about their experiences (Bass and Thorton 1983). Participants are then instructed to write summaries of these books and to compare how their victims' experiences may have been similar to and different from those presented in the book. These summaries are then presented to the group and discussed.

The next step in the process includes viewing videotapes of victims' accounts of their experiences. Following this, offenders are asked to write about their offenses from the victim's perspective. These accounts are then read to the group and discussed.

The next stage of the victim empathy process is to have each offender role play the details of his most recent offense. He begins by assuming his own role as the abuser while another group member role plays the victim as the offense is re-enacted. Afterward, the abuser is required to switch roles and take the role of his own victim. Group members ask questions about the offender's thoughts and feelings as the role-play occurs. This session is videotaped for later individual review with the offender.

In the final stage of the group, offenders may meet with adult survivors of child sexual abuse or rape. Offenders who have not demonstrated empathy are excluded from the meeting. Victims should outnumber offenders. The group should be told that the victims are in control of the session.

Assertiveness Training and Resocialization Skills

There are some child molesters and rapists who manifest un-assertive behavior alternating with rage. Because they fail to nego-tiate their needs in an assertive manner, they respond to repeated frustration either by turning to children for nurturance and sup-port or by exploding with rage. A useful adjunct to treatment is to teach offenders basic assertive skills such as refusing and mak-ing requests, expressing negative emotions, solving problems, and resolving conflicts. Broader communication skills such as express-ing positive and tender feelings, accepting compliments, initiating conversations, and dating can also be taught.

Family Skills

In cases where it is indicated, family skills may be taught through family therapy groups and marital counseling with spouses. Issues of sexual abuse are opened up and talked about in the family. A basic assumption of the family-systems approach is that the offender's sexually-abusive behavior is part of a larger system of interpersonal interaction within the family, and the in-teraction and relationships between family members affect and are affected by the abusive behavior. Therefore, the functioning of the whole family system and its various subsystems — marital, parent-child, and sibling — should be addressed. A second as-sumption is that the family's functionality needs to be restored, and a safe and nurturing environment needs to be established.

Incest families tend to be significantly more socially isolated, more dependent upon external organizing systems such as church, work, military, more chaotically organized internally, and have higher moral-religious emphasis than normal families. The perpetrator-victim dyad is a controlling force in the family system to which other family members and subsystems accom-modate. There tends to be a strong emotional coalition between perpetrators and victims, and nonabused siblings often occupy an outsider role in the family (Saunders et al. 1987).

Chemical Use and Abuse Groups

Many sex offenders have histories of alcohol and drug abuse. It makes sense to address these abusive behaviors which tend to disinhibit social controls. Single-focus peer groups led by para-professionals using the Alcoholics Anonymous formats are the most popular. Some offenders try to hide behind substance abuse as an excuse for their sexual offending. The therapist should recognize this as a form of denial (see Chapter 3). Not all persons who become intoxicated or who use other drugs engage in sexual offending.

Relapse Prevention*

The treatment of sex offenders is aimed not at "curing" the offender but at helping the person control his or her behavior. This concept of control involves the active participation of the offender in a behavior-change *process*. It reinforces the fact that continued abstinence from offending requires the offender's continued vigilance. The notion of cure implies that the problem has been resolved and no longer exists. Therefore, the offender is thought to be neither at risk to relapse into previous offending habits nor in need of specific methods for avoiding a reoffense. Control, on the other hand, denotes that the problem is being restrained and curbed. It is not unusual for an offender to believe earnestly he will never offend again, only to be caught by surprise when he finds himself in a tempting predicament that elicits a return of his deviant urges.

Relapse prevention is a cognitive-behavioral model for helping the offender gain control over his behavior and thus prevent the occurrence of a reoffense. This model attempts to help the offender maintain abstinence by identifying the decisions that place him at risk for offending, referred to as **seemingly unimportant decisions (SUDs),** the situations that threaten his sense of self-

*Adapted from Pithers et al. 1988; Nelson et al. 1988; and Marlatt 1982.

control over his sexual behavior **(high-risk situations),** and the cognitive and affective or emotional components in his offense pattern.

Relapse prevention should not be introduced at the beginning of sex-offender treatment, because it may lead an offender to intellectualize his problems (Pithers 1991). Victim empathy, cognitive restructuring of distorted thinking styles, and extinguishing deviant sexual arousal should be introduced before the relapse model is presented.

The goal of any treatment program for sex offenders is, of course, to assist the offender to not reoffend. Specific goals such as modifying deviant sexual arousal patterns, remediating social and sexual skills deficits, improving anger management, heightening empathy toward others, and enhancing self-esteem, serve only as subgoals oriented toward aiding the offender in the ultimate task of abstaining from illicit sexual acts in the future. Empirical evidence suggests that psychological treatment modalities are effective in inducing beneficial behavior modifications, including those in the sexual arena. Unfortunately, short-term benefits often fail to become long-term changes. If successful treatment permanently eliminated deviant sexual preferences, relapse rates of sex offenders would be low. Such is clearly not the case. While reconviction rates for sex offenders are lower than those of the general criminal population, repetition of sex offenses is not an infrequent occurrence.

There may be common behavioral and cognitive components associated with relapse, regardless of the particular addictive substance or behavior involved. Three high-risk situations — negative emotional states, interpersonal conflict, and social pressure — are frequently reported prior to relapses. Many rapists report experiencing intense anger just before relapsing. Pedophiles may more frequently report feeling anxious.

In analyzing precursors, a common sequence of changes that ultimately leads to a sexual offense is frequently found. The first change in the offender's usual ways of functioning is affective or emotional. Offenders typically refer to themselves as "feeling moody" or "brooding." The second alteration involves fantasies of performing the unacceptable sex act. Fantasies are converted into thoughts, often cognitive distortions in the third step of the relapse process. Offenders frequently devise rationalizations for their behaviors that minimize the effects of their soon-to-be-committed acts. These distortions often attribute inaccurate properties to potential victims, effectively dehumanizing women or ascribing adult characteristics to children. As their fantasies and thoughts continue, the offenders engage in a process of passive planning, cognitively refining the circumstances that would permit commission of the sexual offense. This passive planning is often accomplished during masturbatory fantasies. In the final step of the relapse process, the plan is manifested behaviorally.

What determines whether an individual will successfully avoid relapse? First, it is assumed the person experiences a sense of perceived control while maintaining abstinence, and that this perception of self-control grows until the person encounters a high-risk situation. The offender may have participated in a treatment program for several years that incorporated many of the components discussed above. His participation has been regular, and he really believes that his problem is solved. He exits the treatment program and feels good about his new lease on life. Then he confronts a **high-risk situation** (see Figure 4.2), faces a situation that threatens his sense of control, and increases the risk of relapse. This may be the presence of a potential victim, the use of disinhibitors such as alcohol and drugs, negative affective states such as anger or frustration, interpersonal conflict, and rationalizations or justifications for engaging in the illicit sexual behavior. Some offenders have difficulty avoiding or anticipating the high-risk situations in which relapse eventually occurs. Frequently,

Figure 4.2
A Cognitive-Behavioral Model of the Relapse Process

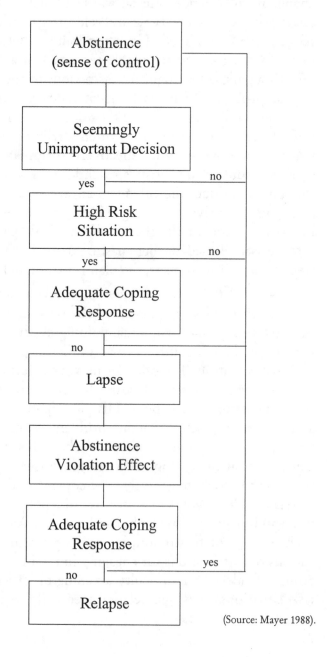

(Source: Mayer 1988).

however, offenders appear to set the stage for their reoffense by covertly seeking out high-risk situations. For example, the abstinent pedophile who decides to become a boy scout leader or the rapist who stops his car in a grocery store parking lot one night as he watches a woman walking to her car alone with her arms full of groceries. Through rationalization and denial the offender places himself in extremely tempting situations which allow him to justify his crime by being overwhelmed and unable to resist the high-risk elements of the circumstances. SUDs can be identified by two primary characteristics: the action appears rational, reasonable, or even worthy of praise, for example, a pedophile volunteering to teach Sunday School at a local church; and the action places the person in a high-risk situation that threatens his continued abstinence (e.g., availability of victims). Therefore, the decision the offender makes only *appears* irrelevant; in fact, it is quite relevant in the process of setting the stage for reoffending.

Once a high-risk situation is encountered, the ability to make an immediate **coping response** decreases the potential for the situation to provoke a relapse, for example, resisting an urge to perform a sexually aggressive act, resolving an argument, or leaving the area where there is so much risk. On the other hand, if a coping response is not made or is unsuccessful, the high-risk situation continues to carry the risk of reoffending. A likely result is a decreased sense of control and a helpless feeling of "It's no use, I can't handle it."

When no effective coping response is produced, the person **lapses** in his abstinence. A lapse refers to a slip or mistake that can be corrected. Control is not completely lost and reoffending does not immediately occur. A lapse is seen as an important process or step than can, but does not necessarily, lead to total relapse. The lapse is the first instance of the forbidden or undesirable behavior. A lapse is often the fantasy of the illicit sexual act, experiencing sexual arousal in response to a deviant theme or object, actively seeking a potential victim, or the initial phases of the seduction of a child. It is a cognitive, affective, or behavioral "red flag" — or danger signal — that a full-blown relapse is imminent. It is the offender's response to the lapse that determines in large measure whether he will return to abstinence or proceed to a re-lapse (reoffense).

Whether a lapse ultimately leads to reoffending depends upon what has been called the **abstinence violation effect (AVE)**. It consists of the cognitive and affective reactions to the occurrence of an initial slip or lapse following a period of absti-nence. The AVE represents the conflict between the offender's previous self-image as an abstainer and his recent experience of the prohibited thought or action. "If I am no longer a sex of-fender, why am I masturbating to fantasies of children?" or "Why am I cruising this campus looking for women who are un-accompanied?" As a result of the AVE, the offender experiences cognitive dissonance, a negative emotional state brought on by the realization that one's beliefs and behaviors are inconsistent over the conflict between his beliefs about himself as an abstainer and his actual conduct. One way to decrease this negative emo-tional state is to engage in behavior that leads to a sexual release (most likely reoffending), but another possibility is to reduce the dissonance by altering one's self-image to bring it in line with the reoccurring behavior, for example, "I guess I will always be a sex offender, and there's no sense fighting it.". Either one of these strategies increases the probability that the lapse will escalate into a full relapse.

Another aspect of the AVE is the tendency to look at a lapse as an indication of personal failure such as lack of willpower, or moral corruption. If the lapse is construed as a personal failure, the offender may begin to expect failure from that point on and decrease his resistance to subsequent lapses. The overall result is an increased probability that a lapse will be followed by a com-plete relapse.

A 35-year-old child molester completed a two-year treatment program in which he received a combination of intensive marital counseling and assertiveness training. His offense pattern of molesting younger girls began when he was a teenager. Upon termination of treatment he considered himself cured and no longer at risk for reoffending. Perhaps because of assorted stressors, after six years his marriage began to deteriorate again. He began to spend increasing amounts of time in community activities that involved his daughter and other children (SUD). He particularly liked the attention and esteem the young children gave him. On several occasions he started supervising the children when no other adults were present (high-risk situation). On one such occasion he started horse-playing physically with one of the girls in a swimming pool. He became sexually aroused and interpreted the child's actions as seductive toward him (lapse). As he became aware of his sexual arousal, he felt ashamed, depressed, and powerless to prevent himself from molesting the child (AVE), which he subsequently did (relapse).

The relapse-prevention model assumes that the sex offender can learn to recognize the sequence or chain of events that precedes a relapse, and can evolve appropriate coping strategies to intervene before it is too late. Offenders come to realize that their offenses are neither isolated nor discrete events. Instead, they are the culmination of a long series of external events, such as access to a victim, interpersonal conflict, substance abuse, internal as well as affective states and cognitions.

The main technique for highlighting this offense sequence or pattern is the development of individualized, detailed cognitive-behavioral offense chains. This is usually best accomplished by starting at the offense in question and moving backward in time, identifying each significant incident preceding the crime. This is first done for the external events; then the cognitive interpretations and emotional responses to those events are added.

This helps the offender to separate his reactions to the events from the events themselves.

In addition to exploring offenses that have already been committed, the offender is asked to create an imaginary situation that could provoke a relapse in the future. In other words, he constructs a guided relapse fantasy. From the chains of both actual and fantasized offenses, SUDs, high-risk situations, coping response failures, lapses, and AVEs are identified.

As the offense chains are developed, the offender becomes more aware of the danger signals that foretell the impending risk for relapse. At each link in the chain, the offender explores interventions at the stimulus control level, such as avoiding pornography, avoiding being alone with a child, avoiding the use of alcohol or drugs, or avoiding access to weapons, and the cognitive level distorted thinking. At each juncture in the offense chain the offender and therapist examine alternative responses that reduce the risk of the immediate situation. Role plays and behavioral rehearsal assignments reinforce and enhance skill in the delivery of these alternative behaviors. In this way, more effective coping responses are programmed.

SUDs are identified by the offender to prevent their covert placement in a high-risk situation. The process of discovering the meaning and purpose of an SUD robs it of justification value for the offense.

Although a major focus of treatment from the relapse prevention perspective is teaching the offender to recognize and intervene early in the relapse chain, this approach also prepares the person to handle the lapse and the associated AVE effectively, if and when it occurs. Central to this preparation is the emphasis that the offender remains at risk for reoffense even after a period of intensive treatment.

In group, an offender can be asked to describe one of his relapse fantasies as well as the precursors, SUDs, and lapses. Sometimes the offender will experience an AVE right in group. This provides a good opportunity to help the offender process his feelings and learn more effective coping strategies for handling AVEs.

One coping technique is to have the offender evaluate the pros and cons of reoffending and abstaining. It forces the person to focus on both the immediate and delayed consequences of both behaviors. Because this discussion occurs before the occurrence of a lapse, the offender can be instructed to refer to the written evaluation of the pros and cons of reoffending versus abstaining as part of a relapse contract.

Another technique that can be employed at the time of a lapse is to have the offender compare the positive effects he expects from engaging in the lapse with its actual effects. If, for example, the lapse is masturbation in response to a deviant fantasy, the offender may contract to list the positive effects he expects will accrue from the lapse, such as sexual gratification, or a sense of power or control. After the lapse the offender would complete a similar list of the actual effects of committing the lapse, such as shame, guilt, low self-esteem. This technique, then, can highlight the offender's unrealistic expectations for the deviant sexual behavior and propel him back toward a state of abstinence.

By preparing the offender for the occurrence of a lapse, the negative self-evaluation and dissonance of the accompanying AVE is reduced. Instead of interpreting the lapse as a sign of weakness, he can attribute it to a predictable part of the abstinence process. A self-statement, such as, "My therapist told me this would happen, and now that it has, I'm glad to have been prepared," can replace such relapse engendering statements as, "Treatment was ineffective and I guess I'll never be able to control my sexual behavior. What's the use of fighting it?"

Another procedure in the relapse-prevention treatment process is to develop a contract with the offender on how to act when confronted with a high-risk situation. For example, if one of the precursors to the offender's reoffending is purchasing pornography, a contract might look like the following.

1. Whenever I feel the urge to look at pornography, I will wait five minutes before acting on that urge. If I then decide to view the pornography, I recognize that I am purposefully deciding to lapse and will be unable to blame my behavior on something else.

2. Before entering the store to purchase the pornography, I will wait 10 minutes.

3. I will only buy one magazine.

4. I will have to turn the magazine over to my probation officer at our next meeting.

5. I have to give an amount equal to the cost of the magazine to the local women's shelter.

When the relapse-prevention model is used with offender groups, the first stage consists of explaining the relapse model (Table 4.2) to the group (Pithers 1991). Once that is done group members are asked to prepare a list of their own risk factors for reoffending. These are then read aloud to the group and a complete listing is constructed. Examples of the risk factors offenders might identify include:

- fear of rejection
- low self-esteem
- rushing into relationships
- emotional isolation
- drug abuse
- negative self statements
- unemployment
- unexpressed anger
- keeping secrets

Table 4.2
Symptoms of Relapse

Changes in Feelings and Attitudes

- Adamant belief that reoffending cannot happen
- Increased fantasizing and obsessive thinking
- Self-centered thinking
- Depression, apathy, and hopelessness
- Feelings of or actual failure or loss
- Self-pity
- Lying and manipulation
- Defensiveness
- Tunnel vision
- Feeling stress build up
- Anger and Irritability
- Denial, minimization, and rationalization
- Anxiety, apprehension
- Boredom

Physical Complaints, Changes, and Problems

- Sleep problems
- Psychosomatic symptoms (e.g., gastric distress, head-aches, backaches, etc.)
- Onset of illness
- Sexual changes or indifference
- Change in appetite

Behavioral Changes

- Significant life changes (e.g., loss of job)
- Impulsive behavior
- Compulsive behavior
- Resumed or increased substance abuse
- Social isolation
- Indifference or avoidance about getting help
- Changes in sex life
- Loss of commitments and/or daily discipline

- drinking alcoholic beverages
- loneliness
- boredom
- overworking
- compartmentalization of one's life experiences
- ending a relationship
- believing you are cured
- use of pornography
- coercing victims with drugs or alcohol
- going to playgrounds or public restrooms

Each member then lists his highest risk factors from the list, and these are shared with the group so that risk factors most common to the entire group are identified. Once this is done, the group works to identify the precursors or cues to signal to the offender that he is in a high-risk situation. For example, if the risk factor is "not feeling good about myself," some of the cues that might help the offender recognize his predicament are

- making cruel comments to others
- feeling angry or frustrated
- engaging in solitary activities
- putting off doing things
- bragging to others.

For each risk factor, the group then identifies potential coping strategies to effectively handle the situation. Privately each offender rates the strategies identified on two dimensions: likelihood of success and ability to use. These are then subsequently discussed in group. Examples of coping strategies that offenders might be asked to evaluate in coping with the high-risk situation of being rejected include:

- talk to someone about how you feel

- look somewhere else for acceptance
- ask the other person to clarify his or her behavior toward you
- accept disappointment.

Unrealistic evaluations of coping strategies are challenged in group meetings.

In the next stage of the group, each member is asked to prepare a reminder card for the group's most common high-risk factor. The name of the high-risk factor is written on one side of an index card. The five most reliable cues and the five optimal coping strategies are written on the other side. Two sets of each card are prepared. The offender keeps one and the other is given to the treatment staff who will periodically ask the offender, both in and out of group, how they would handle the high-risk situation. This helps insure that offenders will regularly review their cards.

The relapse-prevention model seems to work better for pedophiles than it does with rapists (Pithers 1991). This may be due to the fact that there seems to be less time between the fantasy, the SUD, and relapse for rapists than is typically true of pedophiles.

Treating Intellectually Disabled Sex Offenders*

There are more similarities than differences in working with intellectually disabled sex offenders compared to nondisabled sex offenders. Both groups have cognitive and behavioral deficits. They express various levels of denial; possess immature social and sexual skills, leading to helplessness and lack of assertiveness; feel intimidated by peers; experience low self-esteem and high self-criticism; demonstrate inadequate adult heterosexual or homosexual responsiveness; engage in obsessively deviant fantasy patterns; lack empathy; display poor impulse control, particularly in re-

*Adapted from Harven et al. 1990.

Table 4.3
Treatment Components for
Intellectually-Disabled Sex Offenders

1. Family Groups
    - Moral inventory
    - Problem-solving
    - Self-disclosure
    - Accountability
    - Sexual deviancy

2. Workshops
    - Criminal self-talk
    - Anger management
    - Sex education
    - Sexual myths

3. Behavior Contracting

4. Journal writing

5. Self-charting

6. Alcohol/drug abuse

7. Personality disorder treatment

8. Sexual deviancy
    - Arousal control
    - Plethysmograph
    - Cognitive restructuring
    - Minimal arousal conditioning
    - Covert sensitization
    - Aversive behavioral rehearsal

9. Relationship development

(Source: Haaven et al. 1990.)

sponse to stress; and unable to process and evaluate information, especially about sexual roles and sexuality.

Disabled and Nondisabled Sex Offenders

There are three primary differences between intellectually disabled and nondisabled sex offenders.

Denial. Both groups of offenders deny their culpability in varying degrees. Both groups have developed self-serving thought processes justifying their acts. The thinking errors used in the denial process by both groups show the same levels of sophistication.

Once in treatment, however, the two offender groups appear to respond differently when their denial is questioned. Many nondisabled offenders quickly abandon their prior protestations of denial, even though in some cases this may be a superficial response. Intellectually disabled offenders, on the other hand, tend to cling to their justification systems more rigidly. Progress is slow but more likely to be genuine. Denial in intellectually disabled offenders tends to be reduced incrementally.

Coping and Learning Skills

Because intellectually disabled sex offenders have greater difficulty taking care of themselves and solving life crises, they are more dependent on the program and staff. This usually results in better compliance with program rules and a continuing association with the program long after they are free from any legal requirements.

Self-esteem. Both disabled and nondisabled sex offenders suffer from low self-esteem. The nondisabled offenders, however, have a broader range of competencies allowing more positive social interactions. Because disabled offenders have fewer areas of competency, they compensate by exaggerating their accomplishments. This is sometimes seen by others as abrasive and obnoxious. Disabled offenders are sensitive to criticism, overreact to feedback from others, are more fearful of change, and try to hang onto behaviors they have mastered regardless of how maladaptive they are.

Treatment Methods

Effective interventions. Due to misconceptions concerning the inability to change their thinking patterns, *cognitive restructuring* has seldom been used in the treatment of intellectually disabled sex offenders. However, when these methods are adapted to the particular learning problems, they can be quite effective. Using a simple labeling approach, the offender can be taught to associate a particular label with a constellation of behaviors or thoughts, enabling him to identify and associate new thoughts or behaviors with new labels. Thinking errors can also be addressed by using such things as flash cards that have a thinking error inscribed on one side and a rational challenge included on the flip side. For example, "She's smiling at me; she must want to have sex," might be printed on one side of the flash card. The challenge on the flip side might read, "People smile for a lot of reasons. She is just being pleasant and is probably not thinking about having sex at all." Complex behaviors and cognitive processes are simplified, reduced to labels, and presented both verbally and in pictures. Insight training requiring the client to use inductive and deductive reasoning should be de-emphasized.

Minimal arousal conditioning. This method teaches offenders early recognition of their sexually deviant arousal and how to intervene effectively in these patterns, has been used effectively with these offenders. Intellectually disabled offenders describe actual events they found sexually exciting. Then the therapist writes a script that the offender reads or recites into a tape recorder daily. He sniffs ammonia fumes whenever he is aware of arousal and then begins to read the script from the beginning again. *Covert sensitization* (see this

Chapter's earlier discussion) has also been found to be effective with disabled offenders.

Plethysmography. This has been used effectively with intellectually disabled offenders. When adapted for these offenders, it can help to focus treatment on deviant arousal and deviant behaviors, instead of getting sidetracked by the myriad of interrelated problems these offenders present.

Interventions with limited application. *Individual counseling* is usually not a method of choice because these clients may try to manipulate the therapist or use the personal attention they get in individual treatment to impress their fellow offenders. However, if an offender has a specific problem that is not being adequately addressed in group treatment, individual therapy may be prescribed. In these instances it should focus on specific goals, it should be time-limited, examples include clarifying the group process, helping the offender fit into the group, addressing regression, and grieving issues. Sometimes helping the offender work through his own sexual victimization is also done in individual therapy.

When alternative methods are ineffective in correcting sexual obsessiveness, *medical interventions* may be introduced. Low doses of Mellaril (an antipsychotic drug that decreases aggression, causes secondary impotence, and is used to treat thought and mood disorders) and depo-provera are used to control hypersexuality. Neither of these options provides a miracle solution. Occasionally, introducing a pharmacological intervention may cause an offender to act out sexually to compensate for the partial loss in sexuality. Of the two medications, some experts report that Mellaril seems to be the more effective with this offender population.

Card sorts (described earlier) are useful in assessing denial. They do not correlate well with either known histories of offense or measured sexual arousal, but they may be useful as reference points.

Ineffective interventions. *Masturbation satiation* has not proven effective with disabled sex offenders perhaps because the procedure requires complicated fantasy switching. It may also be that offenders with organic syndromes do not reach sexual satiation easily.

Empathy training has not proven to be effective with intellectually disabled offenders either. Traditionally, programs teach empathy training by showing videotapes of former victims describing the abuse-related difficulties they experienced as children and adults. Many disabled offenders may become sexually aroused from viewing these tapes.

Although differences in treating disabled and nondisabled sex offenders exist, adapting some of the procedures usually used in nondisabled-offender treatment for disabled ones can lead to improvements. Intellectually disabled offenders respond to teaching that is concrete, repetitive, and respects their humanity.

The Social Skills Program at the Oregon State Hospital is one innovative program that has had some success in treating disabled offenders. It incorporates an intensive residential treatment model with a variety of specialized aftercare arrangements in supervised dorms, sheltered housing, and community placements. The inpatient phase uses a modified therapeutic community approach.

Treating Female Sex Offenders*

The goals of treatment with female sex offenders are not too different from those for male offenders.

1.   Assume full responsibility for the sexually abusive behavior;

2.   Increase empathy for the of the sexual abuse victim(s)

---

*Adapted from Matthews et al. 1989.

3. Become aware of the behavioral patterns that led to the crime and significantly change those patterns to prevent further offending.

The treatment modality most frequently used seems to be group psychotherapy. The issues the group discuss include:

- Sexual abuse and sexual offending;
- Male dependency;
- Self-worth.

Female offenders explore together the relationship between their own victimization, if applicable, and experiences with betrayal by adult figures and their subsequent sex crimes. By addressing their memories and feelings surrounding their own victimization, they come to realize how profoundly their own self-images and behavior have been shaped by those experiences. This can help them appreciate the inappropriateness of their offenses and the impact it had on their victims. Some women learn to make important boundary distinctions.

> "I've learned to recognize where the boundaries between acceptable touching and unacceptable touching lie. What I previously told myself was not sexual abuse I now realize was abuse. Having my kids witness any sexual act can be devastating to them and lead to all kinds of confusion and fears."

Male-dependency issues are common with female sex offenders and helping women understand these should be an important part of treatment. Discussing sex role differences between men and women and ways to change traditional views should be discussed. The treatment focus is to empower the women — to help them see themselves as increasingly self-sufficient and worthy of respect.

Many female sex offenders have a deep sense of shame as a result of the abuse they experienced and, in turn, perpetrated. Feeling accepted and understood, these women are enabled to come to terms with their past and recent experiences.

Summary

Sexual offending is not a "sickness." A treatment model based on a "sickness" model is outdated and probably based on false assumptions. An examination of sex offenders' behavior reveals that these people are not out of control. To the contrary, their offending behavior is well controlled. They typically work very hard to set up situations that enable them to offend, or they knowingly allow such circumstances to unfold. This merely means that these individuals have in their behavioral repertoires various responses, including sexual abuse and assault, that prior to treatment at least, are highly likely to occur when preceding behavioral circumstances are in place.

Consistent with this view of sex offenders is a treatment program that trains them to reduce exposure to risky situations, to alter their views in a prosocial direction, to develop alternative, more acceptable responses to meet their needs, and to provide them with the skills necessary to enact these alternatives. Treatment, then, is seen as training or education rather than therapy per se, and it is not counted as a "cure." Chronic sexual deviation is a robust disposition, highly resilient, and resistant to alteration. This means that the offender is seen as continuing to be at risk after treatment. The aim of treatment is to reduce that risk and make self-management more effective in controlling unacceptable impulses and behaviors.

5

The Officer and the Treatment Process

In this and the remaining chapters, the emphasis shifts from educating the reader about the nature of sex crimes and sex offenders, and the prescribed treatment modalities to a discussion of issues important to probation and parole officers in managing and supervising sex offenders. From the beginning, there needs to be agreement about community interventions in cases of sex offenses from the point of arrest through the treatment and discharge processes. Each step in the intervention process can provide the supervising officer with valuable information.

The first intervention is the **investigation**. Police, protective service workers and rape crisis center workers need to collaborate in sex offense investigations. Each agency has specific investigative expertise that can assist in bringing the offender to justice. Specialized techniques are needed to effectively handle the child victim, to assess family dynamics, and to address the complicated legal problems posed by the young victim/witness. Police collaboration with sexual assault trauma centers can reduce the victim's physical and emotional trauma. Special handling of evidence is needed for later phases of prosecution. In all sexual assault investigations, detailed reporting of offender and victim behavior is important to the therapist and the supervising officer. Police, protective service, and medical reports will supply information needed to prepare sentencing recommendations, to learn the nature of the offender's deviance, and to break through the offender's denial and minimizing.

The second point of intervention is the **arrest.** Once sufficient evidence exists to arrest a person suspected of a sex offense, the arrest and jailing of that suspect is recommended. This insures that the victim/witness will not be subjected to intimidation by the accused. If the accused is not arrested or is later released, a temporary restraining order should be obtained to establish a provision of no-contact between the accused and the victim. In most cases of intra-family sexual abuse, the accused, not the victim, should be removed from the home. Child protective services should be encouraged to open a case on the family and to provide treatment not only to the child in particular, but also to the other family members. In other cases involving child victims, a Child in Need of Supervision (CHINS) petition should be filed in court on behalf of the child victim to insure treatment for the family and the appointment of an advocate (guardian-ad-litem) for the child. This intervention is particularly important in instances where the family may support the offender's denial.

If warranted by the facts, the third intervention — **charging** — should be pursued. This reinforces the fact that sexual assault and sexual abuse are felonies.

Next in the sequence of interventions is **determination of guilt.** Opinions differ on this point, but the author believes probation should be recommended only to offenders who plead guilty. Such an admission of guilt is a prerequisite for acceptance into treatment and the prospect of profiting from it. Not only is admitting culpability important in the treatment process, it is essential for dispelling the false sense of guilt almost universally experienced by victims. The offender who does not admit guilt is likely to be a continued risk to community safety.

Step five in the process is **disposition**. Imposed sentences are recommended for offenders in cases where

- the victim is severely brutalized by the assault, or
- the number of known offenses is high and suggests a deeply ingrained pattern of assault, or
- the perpetrator does not plead guilty.

Otherwise, for the offender pleading guilty and being placed on probation, special conditions should be spelled out, such as jail time, no-contact provisions while unsupervised with anyone under the age of eighteen (for pedophiles), and successful completion of treatment.

The sixth step in intervention is **supervision**. Successful compliance with court and agency conditions of release depends in large measure upon the adequacy of the supervisory process. This manual is intended to help insure that supervising officers are knowledgeable about the population of sex offenders with which they work and are familiar with the specific strategies that are recommended for follow-up.

The final intervention, for our purposes is **treatment**. The preferred primary mode of treatment for most offenders is group treatment. This may be combined with support group participation (e.g., Parents Anonymous, Sex Addicts Anonymous, Alcoholics Anonymous) and family therapy. Individual therapy is frequently indicated for many of these offenders as well. The responsibility for coordinating these varied treatment approaches rests squarely with the officer.

Probation officers may believe that treatment programs for sex offenders are a resource for persons convicted of felony sex crimes and placed on specialized caseloads. Certainly, the programs that have been described are appropriate for these offenders. Consideration should be given, however, to expanding sex offender treatment to misdemeanor sex offenders as well (e.g., public lewdness, indecent exposure, solicitation of a child). The justification for this recommendation is that sex offenders often commit multiple types of offenses. Offenders arrested and sentenced for misdemeanor sex offenses often admit to having committed felony sex offenses. Many felony sex offenders reveal committing misdemeanor sex offenses prior to the felony arrest. Consequently, referring misdemeanor sex offenders to treatment should assist in deterring and preventing future sexual assaults.

Community attitudes toward the sex offender and the way other agencies and programs handle him affect the officer's supervision of the offender in two ways:

- they shape the offender's attitude toward his deviance and the victim, and

- they shape the offender's attitude toward supervision.

For example, if the prevailing community attitudes toward intra-family child sexual abuse suggest that it is a "private matter" to be handled discretely out of the public eye, or if the district attorney or the police do not handle date rape as a serious matter, the supervising officer's ability to impact the offender's deviant values is compromised. Officers need to learn how others are handling sexual assault. They need to collaborate with other sectors of the community in strategic planning for the whole community. The participants in the coalition will usually include:

- child protective services
- police
- courts
- district attorneys
- public defenders
- defense attorneys
- victim/witness advocacy groups
- mental health professionals
- self-help groups

- institutional program staff
- county jail staff
- community leaders

The Officer's Role in the Treatment Process

As mentioned above, the supervising officer plays a crucial role in coordinating supervision and treatment opportunities. This role, however, is multifaceted.

One part of the officer's role is that of **support**. The offender should view the officer as an advocate for treatment and a colleague in the change process. Sex offenders need added incentive to enter and to complete treatment. During most of their lives, the offenders may have tried to hide their deviant sexual behavior and fantasies from others. Once the shock, embarrassment and humiliation of arrest, trial and conviction have worn off, they often want to forget that anything happened and to return to the pattern of keeping their deviance inside.

Support is needed in several ways. Officers can:

- recommend court-ordered treatment in pre-sentence investigation reports;
- mandate successful completion of treatment in the rules of supervision;
- restrict client's access to high risk situations pending success of therapy (e.g., reunification with family, contact with family, acceptable employment, travel permits, levels of supervision, etc.);
- prepare the offender for treatment by spelling out the goals and impressing upon him the importance of successful completion of treatment; and
- monitor progress in treatment through regular communications with treatment providers.

Another facet of an officer's role is that of a **consultant**. Strategies in changing offender behavior should be linked between the treatment environment and the offender's daily life. The officer can provide this link by observing the offender in his own environment. The officer can watch what is done in treatment (even to the point of sitting in on group sessions) and also observe the offender's daily life. Cues from the offender's personal life may be inconsistent with what he is saying or doing in treatment. Such discrepancies, when brought to the therapist's attention, may be valuable in breaking through the denial system and enhancing the effects of treatment. For example, a child molester who was not very active in group meetings might have a photo album of young children in his residence. Sharing this information with the treatment provider might lead to a polygraph exam to determine whether the offender continues to masturbate to fantasies of molesting children.

This part of the officer's role undermines one of the strongest inducements to continued deviant sex arousal and offending — secrecy. As long as the offender can keep hidden his deviant sexual arousal and fantasizing, he can manipulate the treatment process.

The supervising officer often becomes the central repository to which various concerned parties can forward information about the offender. Consequently, the officer is a valued part of the overall treatment process, because treatment is to be successful when the provider is in the dark about significant aspects of the offender's behavior.

The fourth aspect of the officer's role is that of an **evaluator**. With increasing knowledge and sophistication about the treatment process, the officer can begin to assess the offender's application of treatment in his life. This kind of feedback to the treatment provider can be invaluable in assessing progress.

Finally, the officer functions as an **enforcer**. As enforcer, the officer holds the offender accountable for his behavior. This enforcement includes imposing the known consequences for behavior. Enforcement teaches accountability and responsibility.

This role description for the officer underscores the importance of information — sharing between treatment providers and supervising officers. This requirement, however, often conflicts with a treatment provider's concerns about protecting the client's **confidentiality**. Although this is understandably an important ethical issue, the reality of treatment and supervision of the sex offender make it impossible for a confidential relationship to exist between therapist and offender. Confidentiality will prevent the treatment team from obtaining the information they need to make sure that the offender does not return to his offense pattern. Confidentiality is the curtain of secrecy that makes it more likely that the offender will act out. Consequently, external controls are required to help insure community safety while the offender is treated on an out-patient basis.

Prior to entering treatment, the offender should be advised that limited confidentiality is a consequence of belonging to the program. The offender should be asked to sign an agreement that limits confidentiality (see example of a consent form in Appendix C) as a precondition to entering the treatment program. With limited confidentiality, the therapist can contact the supervising officer. If employers need to be contacted, the supervising officer should do so. If parents, spouse or family members need to be spoken to, that too can be done. Confidentiality is said to be limited, rather than eliminated, because no one may be contacted without a reason. The offender is still protected against casual and unnecessary release of information about him. During the course of supervision, it may be necessary to obtain additional releases from the offender as his life circumstances change or as more information is obtained about his offense patterns.

Some question whether the officer's law enforcement role will inhibit the offender from free discussion of fantasy, cognitive distortions, arousal patterns, and other sexual subjects. The question underscores a basic distinction between the types of activities the therapist performs and those the officer performs. The primary area of concern for the treatment provider is the extent to which the offender is relating to himself and his deviance. On the other hand, the officer's primary responsibility arises from the mandate of the court and the policies of the department with respect to the offender's sexual behavior. The officer's activities are spelled out in the court orders, the statutes, and the administrative rules of the agency.

In cases with court-ordered treatment differences of opinions about confidentiality or other issues between officer and therapist, the court should be approached to decide whether the treatment is acceptable. In cases of disagreement between officer and therapist in agency-mandated treatment, resolving the differences should be accomplished through administrative review.

Treatment of the sex offender demands that the offender be truthful. However, information can become problematic to the officer and the therapist. Mandatory reporting comes into play if the offender reveals unreported incidents about:

- sexual behavior with a child under 16,
- involvement in producing or distributing child pornography,
- involvement in child prostitution.

The revelation must be specific enough to pinpoint a person through name, time, and place. The officer must report such incidents to child protective services or to law enforcement, so that the victim can be treated. This obligation stands for acts committed either before or after conviction. If the offender reveals violations of the current supervision, these must be reported to the officer and disposed of with the officer's supervisor.

Some sex offenders have reservations about being completely "above board" about their undiscovered sex offenses during their participation in treatment because they fear that such information could be used against them in any revocation proceeding. One way to address this concern is to suggest that the offender avoid giving specifics of prior occurrences, such as the names, sex, age, place and time of those offenses. In any event, probation and parole officers should work out a standard explanation of the implications of offender revelations. This should be reviewed during the initial interview (see Table 5.1) so that the offender realizes the full impact of future statements made to the officer or therapists.

Offenders who are being supervised should also be advised that they have the right to remain silent during questioning by the supervising officer. The right to avoid self-incrimination applies to an offender who is on probation or parole. This is particularly applicable to offenses or violations committed while on probation or parole. For example, during an interview the offender begins to divulge information that may lead to an arrest. The officer should interrupt the offender and give the Miranda warning. The officer must decide whether the offender will be permitted to leave the office or whether an arrest will be ordered. Certainly if an arrest is planned, the offender should be Mirandized.

Sex Offender Treatment *v.*
Other Forms of Treatment

It is common to seek a mental health provider by seeing who has the largest Yellow Pages ad in the phone directory, or who has the best reputation in the community. Unfortunately, these criteria may not identify the professionals who are qualified to provide specialized treatment services for sex offenders. The

Table 5.1
Implications of Offender Revelations

You are beginning supervision for a sex offense conviction. If you have not already done this, it is important that you:

- fully admit your involvement in the convicting offense,

- disclose your history of sexual development and behaviors,

- discover and begin discussing what arouses you sexually and what you do when aroused.

You need to be aware, however, that if you reveal some crimes, your supervising officer may be required to report them to authorities.

1. If you reveal having sexual behavior with someone under 16 years of age and from your revelation that person can be identified, your officer must discuss the incident with child protective services, the sheriff's department, or the city police, so the victim can receive treatment.

2. If you reveal having involvement in child pronography or child prostitution, and from your revelation that individual can be identified, your officer must again take the same action.

3. If your officer asks you to account for your whereabouts or activities during any period following your conviction, the rules of supervision obligate you to truthfully and completely provide this information to your officer.

4. If you reveal law violations committed after your conviction, violations of court-ordered conditions, or violations of the rules of supervision, your officer needs to clarify these with you and determine their disposition. You need to be aware that your therapist will be working with your officer. What you say to your therapist will be shared with your officer when appropriate, and what you say to your officer will be shared with your therapist.

reasons for this vary, but essentially revolve around the significant differences between treating sex offenders and other patients.

Mandated treatment does not have a good reputation in mental health circles because of the less-than-positive outcomes therapists have experienced. Offenders with no motivation are traditionally referred by the court for treatment. Often the offender comes to treatment but denies all wrongdoing (see discussion of denial in Chapter 3). Weeks or months pass with the offender only talking about the unfairness of the system and his belief that he was railroaded. Frequently, he stops coming altogether because there is no way to force him to continue for this reason many clinicians refuse to take mandated clients. Little if any benefit is derived. If mandated treatment is going to work, there must be collaboration among the parties involved. The therapist must also insist that the offender admit his offenses (see discussion about interviewing sex offenders in Chapter 3). It is a good idea to have the offender sign the treatment contract (see example in Appendix N), which outlines treatment requirements in court at the time of sentencing. Failure to comply with the rules of treatment or failure to attend sessions is reported to the supervising officer who should then counsel the offender about his options or proceed with a revocation hearing. Under these conditions, sex offenders can often be kept in treatment long enough to benefit from it. The treatment agreement inhibits the offender's freedom to exit treatment whenever the urge to molest or to assault re-emerges.

Another way in which standard therapy and sex offender treatment differ is in terms of **setting treatment goals**. In the usual case, goal-setting is a joint process between the therapist and the patient. In fact, the patient usually has the final say in this matter. However, it is not possible to let the sex offenders set the goals of treatment. Typical offenders are often more afraid of losing their compulsion to offend than they are of keeping it. They will try to appear cooperative with treatment but will have surreptitious goals (e.g., return home as soon as possible, get therapist to agree that they don't really need to be in treatment, get the officer to support their belief that the victim did not tell the truth, convince the officer how they are the real victims). Unlike other forms of therapy, the treatment provider must be clear from the start what the goal of treatment is. The primary goals are to learn to control the unacceptable behavior and to stop offending.

Therapists do not usually try to **communicate values.** Their training teaches them how to be "neutral" with clients and not to impose their values on others. With sex offenders, however, this approach is ineffective. In fact, the therapist who uses this methods runs the risk of colluding with the addiction. Sex offenders usually try to minimize the impact of their behavior. No alcohol or drug counselor would spend much time discussing with a client whether alcohol or drugs were harmful. The danger is a given and they treat any other stance on the part of the client as denial.

Therapists typically dislike playing policeman. Usually, their patients come to them voluntarily, and the therapist has no power to tell them to do anything. **Setting limits** with no power to enforce them is a sure way to fail with a sex offender. If a therapist should try to control a client's behavior, the attempt invites a power struggle the counselor cannot win. If a client is ambivalent about his behavior, a therapist who tries to control the ambivalence is likely to cause the client to take a more forceful position. This approach may actually increase the chances that the client will act out.

Not unexpectedly, therapists will apply the skills learned with other clients to the treatment of sex offenders. Consequently, a therapist inexperienced in treatment of sex offenders may bristle at the suggestion that he or she set limits. However, this limit setting is a cornerstone for such treatment. Information obtained from supervising officers, the child's therapist (in incest cases), from the spouse and others contributes to determining what kinds of limits are needed (e.g., "You have been seen sitting in your car alone for long periods of time in the shopping center parking lot where your offense of record was committed. This absolutely has to stop or you will be back talking to the judge.")

Limiting confidentiality was discussed above, but the reader needs to realize that the difference between the treatment of sex offenders and other kinds of treatment is an important one. Many mental health professionals see requests from the child protection agency, from probation and parole, even from the courts as invasive and anti-therapeutic. As stated above, however, sex offenders use confidentiality to protect the deviancy and to manipulate treatment personnel. Often sex offenders will argue that the alternative to entering the treatment program is incarceration and that the offender is, therefore, being coerced into signing a limited confidentiality contract. The answer to this is that the legal consequence of the offender's behavior is jail. Were the program not available, that is what the offender would get. The program is an alternative for those who qualify; it is a privilege, not a right.

The **withholding of trust** is another major difference between therapy for sex offenders and other forms of therapy. Many would characterize traditional client-therapist relationships as built on trust. Because of the secrecy that is so characteristic of sex offending and because of the propensity to deny culpability, trust is usually not warranted in treating sex offenders.

Sex offenders frequently **appeal to narcissism** by trying to split the treatment team into opposing factions. An offender will assure a clinician that she/he is the only one who understands him, and that the other therapist just does not understand sex offenders. If the therapist is influenced by this kind of conniving, he/she will begin to collude with and protect the offender from the attempts of other professionals to set limits.

Working as a team in the treatment of sex offenders refers to networking of collateral information sources. Without such contacts, the therapist is dependent upon the client's self-report, which is obviously a risky situation. A more appropriate plan is to meet regularly, as a treatment team of supervising officers, child protective services, other therapists, and the family.

Confrontation occurs on some level in every form of therapy, but not nearly to the degree that it should in sex offender therapy. **Confrontation is an ongoing part of sex offender treatment.** The goal of this confrontation is not to release hostility but to maintain rapport with the offender while confronting him about his behavior (e.g., "Hold on there. If you really didn't do it, tell it to the judge. This group is not a court of law, and we will not retry this case in this group. Many of the people here are sincerely interested in overcoming their problems. We don't have time to waste on the story about being railroaded by the system.")

How to Choose a Treatment Provider

An officer who has a sex offender on his/her caseload may not be familiar enough with the mental health resources in the community to know to whom to refer the offender for treatment. Potential sources of information about treatment providers in your area who might be qualified to work with sex offenders include judges, district attorneys, rape-crisis centers, school district administrators, child protective services offices, the local office of the Department of Mental Health and Mental Retardation, and organizations such as Parents Anonymous. Yellow Page directories list treatment providers under the headings of Psychologists, Physicians — Psychiatry, Social Workers, and Psychotherapists.

In the past several years, a number of states, including Washington, Texas, Colorado, and Iowa, have developed a specialty certification or licensure for providers of treatment for sex offenders. In order to qualify for this certification or licensure, providers must meet criteria relating to academic degrees, current licensure, number of hours of specialized training and number of hours or years spent treating sex offenders. Although this information aids the supervising officer in finding appropriate providers in his/her area, it should only serve as a starting point for more detailed evaluation.

It is a good idea to inquire about a potential therapist's experience in working with mandated or resistant clients. Although it is preferable that their experience is with sex offenders, more important is whether they have worked with resistant clients.

Another question for a therapist is whether she/he is willing to communicate with the officer and to what degree. Get it spelled out in terms of a specific release form (see Appendix O).

Is the therapist teachable or does she/he exude an air of omniscience, believing her/himself to be the only true change agent? Does the therapist respect your experience and authority?

Does the therapist have a clear sense of the junctures at which community safety is at risk with a sex offender, and is she or he willing to communicate those concerns to the officer?

Inquire about the evaluation process the therapist uses. If the method is haphazard, the treatment is likely to be haphazard. Ask whether he or she uses a plethysmograph and/or a polygraph in the assessment and monitoring process. If not, how does he or she handle the denial system?

Many therapists are convinced that the offender should pay at least a part of the costs of treatment in order to help insure the offender's investment in the treatment process. Judges can be asked at sentencing to require that the offender pay for treatment as a condition of probation.

The officer will want to avoid treatment providers who talk about "cures." Such references suggest that the persons are naive and unskilled in treating this population. Another group to avoid are religious leaders who focus treatment on spiritual conversion or "anointment," rather than changes in behavior over time. Providers who do not offer group counseling are unlikely to be maximally effective in changing the offender's behavior. In smaller communities, however, this desirable characteristic of treatment programs is sometimes impractical because there may be insufficient numbers of offenders to comprise a group. Finally, officers will want to be skeptical of "quick fix" programs. Providers who talk about ten- or fifteen-week programs may again be reflecting their limited understanding of sex offenses and the persons who commit them.

The supervising officer should ask prospective treatment providers if they are willing to testify in court. The officer should feel free to inquire about the provider's training and experience in treating these kinds of offenders. Ask about the components of the proposed treatment program. How does the provider evaluate the receptivity of a person to treatment? What is the provider's perception of the role of the officer in the treatment process? Are self-help groups used as adjuncts to the treatment program (i.e., substance abuse groups, etc.)? Finally, ask what the provider charges for each of the services he or she offers and what he or she does about indigent offenders.

In some areas of the state, there may be insufficient treatment resources available to the supervising agency. In that case, the local and state agencies in the community that handle sex offenders might consider developing an in-house treatment resource by collectively hiring a treatment specialist to process and treat such offenders. Failing that, supervising officers may need to increase the level of supervision provided to these offenders (see supervision techniques discussed in Chapter 7).

Monitoring Progress

Because sex offenders are at times unreliable informants regarding lapses, it becomes important to use other methods of gaining access to information about their functioning. In order to enhance community safety, an **external supervisory dimension** of the relapse-prevention model should be considered. This dimension improves monitoring by supervising officers by having them **focus on specific offense precursors.** It also increases the efficiency of supervision by **creating an informed network of collateral contacts** to assist in monitoring the offender's behavior (see discussion of collateral information in Chapter 3). Furthermore, the external supervisory dimension encourages a **collaborative relationship between the officer and the treatment providers.**

By specifying an offender's seemingly unimportant decisions, high risk situations, and offense precursors (see discussion of relapse prevention in Chapter 4), the officer is provided with identifiable indicators of the impending danger of relapse. Because officers monitor specific risk factors that are related to the offender's sexual offenses (rather than attempting to keep an eye on all of his behaviors, many of which have little bearing on his tendency to reoffend), efficiency in the officer's performance is increased. Whenever the officer detects or is informed about the presence of an offense precursor, he or she will be able to determine if the sex offender is experiencing a relapse. Because offense precursors appear most commonly in a distinct sequence — that is, emotion, fantasy, cognitive distortion, plan, act — the type of precursor exhibited provides an indication of the imminence of potential relapse. With this type of information, the supervising officer may determine the type of intervention required (e.g., additional conditions of probation/parole, consultation with offender's therapist, probation/parole revocation).

No one officer can provide the amount of supervision that is necessary. Using collateral contacts in the supervision process can help. The offender is asked to name a specified number of friends who would "work to keep him out of jail." Those named must be acceptable to the officer (i.e., no criminal records, no reputation for shady dealings, etc.). Needless to say, persons who do not believe the offense was committed by the offender cannot be expected to be vigilant.

The duties of collateral contacts must be precisely specified. For example, they may be asked to ride in the car with the offender when he rides to and from work. Other community members may be asked to supervise visitation either with the victim or with nonabused siblings.

An important aspect of the external supervisory dimension of relapse prevention entails the instruction of collateral contacts on the principles of relapse prevention. As many members of the collateral network as possible (e.g., spouse, employer, co-workers, friends) should be informed about apparently irrelevant decisions, high risk situations, lapses, the abstinence-violation effect, and offense precursors (i.e., relapse prevention model). In the offender's presence, network members should be encouraged to report lapses to the officer or therapist. Not all potential collateral contacts may be able to serve in this capacity. A spouse who has been a victim of severe beatings by her husband may understandably be reluctant to disclose information for fear of being hurt again. Similarly, wives who are overdependent on their husbands may be reluctant to risk providing any information that could potentially get their husbands into trouble. Employers who value the compulsive work habits of some offenders may be reluctant to report information for fear of losing a good employee.

Using collateral informants in the supervision process gives the supervising officer better information about the offender's work and leisure-time pursuits. A sex offender who is busy is less likely to be preoccupied with deviant fantasies and with scheming to get access to victims than an offender who has extensive leisure time on his hands. In other cases, however, the offender may be a workaholic. An increase in work hours can be as significant as a decrease. The reason for monitoring work as well as leisure time is that work can be and often is used as a way to gain access to victims or to further the deviancy in some manner. For example, a convenience store clerk may spend work time leafing through the adult magazines in order to feed his rape fantasies.

Supervision by collaterals allows outside verification of treatment compliance (see Appendix Q — Partner Alert List). Is the offender abiding by the terms of the treatment contract (e.g., no alcohol or drug use, no unsupervised driving or cruising)?

Monitoring treatment progress is a role jointly shared by the treatment providers and the officer. This task is complicated by the fact that there is no checklist, no test, and no single criterion that can be employed. Some group treatment programs do have evaluation forms, which are periodically completed by participants, that attempt to objectify the evaluation process (see example in Appendix L).

Attendance at individual and group therapy sessions is one useful measure of progress. Needless to say, people are unlikely to receive the help they need if they do not attend therapy sessions. Treatment providers can be asked to verify attendance and notify the officer of absences. When an offender misses a therapy session because of a schedule conflict, he is saying, in effect, that the other business is more important than learning how not to reoffend and is, therefore, a measure of how seriously he takes his problem.

Other measures of treatment compliance and/or progress include participation in group, conscientious completion of homework assignments, overcoming denial (see Chapter 4), understanding of the offense chain and the requisite interventions, assertiveness and willingness to help other group members, emotional understanding of the impact of the offenses, and change of behavior. Behavior change is the goal of treatment, not increased knowledge or even a change of sentiment. Emotional states change, and an offender who cries today for the pain of his victim, may be feeling something quite different tomorrow when the desire to reoffend returns. Officers and therapists must carefully watch for behavior in offenders that reveals internal states that are discrepant with the professed attitudes, feelings and behavior of the offender. When actions and words differ, the more reliable source of information is usually how the person is behaving. An offender who cries about the wedge he drove between his wife and his daughter, but who tells his daughter that he cannot come home yet because his wife will not let him, is continuing the same abusive dynamics.

Offenders in treatment must make progress in all of the areas above in order to continue in treatment. Those who fail to make progress should be referred to the court (especially if the treatment contract was signed before the sentencing judge). If an offender passively attends all of the treatment sessions, should be warned in writing about what he is failing to do and told specifically what must change. He should be given a stated period of time to make the changes. If he does not change his behavior, he should be terminated from the program in writing. The reasons for termination should be specified.

6
The Presentence Investigation

The Offense: The Official Version

Obtaining a concise narrative of what happened in the offense is an important step in developing a useful presentence investigation report. In addition to criminal complaints, use police and social service reports, if available, to establish as much detail about the offense as possible. Among the critical elements needed in the official offense description are the time the offense was first reported and how it was reported. It is necessary to include a statement of the relationship between the offender and the victim. If this is a family relationship, specify the exact nature of the relationship (e.g., natural father, step-father, friend of the family, foster parent, etc.).

Among the most important elements are a description of the specific behaviors of the offender and victim, including descriptions of how access was gained to the victim and what specific sexual behavior occurred. A careful review of the official reports will often reveal information about the offender that, in turn, reflects sexual orientation, fantasies, rituals, level of planning, and any cognitive distortions that may be evidenced in the offender's behavior. The factors that led to the offense should be investigated and described as completely as possible. Include any evidence of the offender's moods, conflicts, and actions that may be related. Sexual acting out sometimes is a reaction to non-sexual problems.

If there has been a reduction of charge due to plea bargaining or other factors, include the original charge and any lesser charges that may have been included. If information has been developed on similar offenses that are not charged, that information may also be included if it is in the official documents.

The Offender's Version

Following the official version of the offense should be a statement of the offender's description of what happened. It should provide the reader with a sense of the offender's level of denial, his view of the victim, and the justifications he has used for his behavior. A basic starting point is to ask the offender to tell what happened in the offense. Follow that statement with questions about why the offense occurred. Ask the offender to repeat his version several times. The offender should be able to relate some of the factors that led to the offense, including feelings, thoughts and fantasies before, during and after the offense occurred. Common feelings include anxiety, depression, and anger. The offender should be asked about any substance use before or during the offense. The kinds and the amounts of substances used, along with the time frame in which they were taken, should be listed.

An important part of the offense is the offender's preoffense activities. Ask about such activities as viewing or reading pornographic materials, sexual or violent fantasies, or plans formulated to carry out the offense. Determine if there were any interpersonal conflicts the offender was having prior to the time of the offense. Ask about such activities as "cruising," isolating the victim, or stalking the victim.

Is the offender admitting to anything that was not already known from other sources? If not, he may be trying to deceive or manipulate the interviewer.

Determine if there was a plea and why the plea was entered. Be aware that some pleas are made specifically to avoid the stigma of a sex offense conviction.

Information should be gathered from the offender about his relationship with the victim. Ask about previous inappropriate sexual activity with the victim and any past or current inappropriate sexual activity with others. As these experiences are discussed, look for patterns of feelings, thoughts, fantasies, and actions that may help to understand the offender. Inappropriate sexual activity in early childhood may be an important indicator of current sexual maladjustments.

Determine the offender's feeling about this offense, his conviction, the victim and the victim's family. If he is open, he may reveal his method of accessing the victim and the fantasy and arousal patterns that led to the victimization. The usual response is to describe the offense as an isolated incident which will never happen again, a "set-up" by the victim or the victim's family, or a misunderstanding. The officer needs to challenge these explanations. This can be achieved by reviewing details of the victim statement with the offender and by reminding him that while the shame and the shock of discovery might have reduced his deviant sexual arousal, the pattern probably will be repeated. For these reasons, the offender needs to be encouraged to begin or to continue in treatment, and to take the offense seriously. This section of the report should also outline any steps the offender might have already taken to change. If the offender reports entering therapy or joining a support group, gather complete information about the treatment program. If the sex crime involved other perpetrators, include their versions of the offense in this section of the investigation report.

Sometimes an offender will demonstrate very good memory for personal-history information, but claim he cannot remember details of the offense or his sexual history. This discrepancy should be confronted.

Victim's Description of the Offense

In the presentence investigation report, the victim's information serves several valuable purposes. It identifies to the offender the trauma caused by his crime and can serve to highlight the offender's points of denial and minimizing. It suggests what is needed to make the community "whole" following the crime. Most important, it offers the victim a voice in the sentencing process. Police and social services reports will usually be the most helpful source of data about the victim. As much this data as possible should be gathered from the official documents so as to limit the need for lengthy questioning of the victim. Among the pertinent data needed are the victim's age, gender, physical appearance, and maturity.

In addition to the descriptive data about the victim, the victim's version of the offense should be sought. If it is appropriate to do so, discrepancies in the offender's version may be discussed with the victim to resolve any differences. The types of behaviors and actions that the offender denies may be very important in understanding his offense and behavioral patterns. The victim may be able to provide that information. The relationship between the victim and offender should be examined. Of particular interest are the offender strategies and actions to access the victim.

A Caution About the Victim's Sensitivity. The officer will encounter many reactions when obtaining statements from victims, and he/she must be alert to avoid inappropriate and insensitive statements or behaviors that may hinder the victim's recovery. It is important to remember that repeated intrusion into the victim's life by the various concerned parties of the criminal justice system and the victim-recovery services can cause the victim additional trauma (sometimes referred to as secondary victimization). For this reason, every effort should be made to reduce the number of people to whom victims have to repeat the details of the crime. On the other hand, the law invites victims to state their wishes concerning disposition of the cases in which they are involved. Sometimes, the act of making themselves heard can be part of the victim's healing process. Victim/witness programs or protective services will often provide the officer with suggestions about the most effective way to gain input from the victim. Officers are encouraged to collaborate in their information gathering efforts with these service providers.

Steps to minimize trauma to victims during the officer's contact include: (1) explaining the purpose of the interview, especially when asking about details of the offense; (2) explaining what is happening with the victim's case in the legal system at that point in time; and (3) inviting the victim to have a supportive person present during the interview process. If the victim is a minor, the parent/guardian needs to be contacted. Other family members may be helpful in supplying information too. If the child is too young, or if it would be inappropriate to interview the child, the officer should try to obtain the information from the parent. In intra-family abuse cases, the officer may encounter situations where the mother sides with the offender against the child victim, or the mother may minimize the seriousness of the offense. Sometimes the victim may take a similar stance. These are very difficult situations to manage, and the officer needs to describe them in the report so this information is available for future management of the case.

Finally, there will be cases in which contact might be inappropriate, when victims decide against making a statement, or when the officer's inquiries are not answered. In these cases, efforts to obtain the statement should be documented, and the reasons for not having the statement noted. Statements available from other reports should be included.

In sex offender cases, the presentence investigation uncovers information about the offender that is used by the court, the institution, the officer, treatment personnel, administrators, and possibly even researchers. The purpose of the presentence investigation is to analyze risks and needs. The investigation results in a basic description of the convicting offense, the harm to the victim and the victim's reaction, community reaction, the offender's version of the offense, and the background of the offender. It points out the offender's level of denial at the time of the interview, sexual history, some initial information about sexual orientation, cognitive distortions about victims, level empathy for the victim, and attitude toward treatment. Finally, presentence investigation reports provide a sentencing recommendation and suggest court-ordered conditions for a treatment and supervision program.

Most of the information in the standard presentence investigation report also is required in the sex offender report. Instead of focusing on the routine details that are normally included, this chapter will highlight the details and the requirements that may be unique to sex crimes and sex offenders.

Personal History of the Offender

Sex offenders usually are very traditional and stable in the areas of educational and employment. Because these areas are often nonthreatening to the offender, they provide a good place to begin the interview.

Educational History

Educational history should be included, as it is in any presentence investigation report. Particular attention should be paid to changes in schools that may reflect sexual problems or offenses. Some offenders have a history of abrupt departures from school and vocational programs that coincide with sex crimes or detection of sexual deviance. A check of school records may reflect the reasons for sudden changes in schools.

Employment History and Background

A complete employment history that accounts for the types and dates of work, locations, and reasons for changes will offer valuable information if there is a connection between employment and deviant sexual behavior. Complete and accurate data (with inquiry from past or present employers, if appropriate) will be important to support recommendations to the court or rules regarding restrictions on type of employment. The offender's choice of employment should be assessed to determine his access to past or future sexual victims. Obviously, a pedophile who continually seeks employment as a teacher, youth counselor, or similar position is a problem. Information should also be gathered on any volunteer positions the offender may have held. Many sex offenders use opportunities to volunteer for programs that provide access to victims.

The officer also needs to be alert to the offender who has a history of overwhelming himself with pressures of work (i.e., workaholic) and who has insufficient relaxation outlets. In some offenders, the anxiety and the pressures of overwork serve as a trigger for deviant sexual behavior.

Something else to look for in examining an offender's work history are instances of underemployment. This may be related to the opportunities such employment provide for access to victims. Alternatively, underemployment may contribute to low-key, chronic anger that can help trigger sex offenses.

Inquire about the offender's relationships with supervisors and colleagues. Is there any evidence of suppressed hostility or open conflicts with these people?

Some offenders may show a pattern of consistent employment but frequent shifting from one place of employment to another. What accounts for this? Does the offender become quickly bored? Are there frequent conflicts with other employees?

Military

Sometimes, the type of military discharge or patterns of assignments within the military reflect sexual problems. Disciplinary actions by the military against the offender may also provide clues to prior offense or adjustment patterns.

Residential History

A careful residential history may show a pattern connected with an offender's deviant behavior. If the residency pattern (e.g., frequent and abrupt moves) suggests possible problems, follow-up with local police departments, child protective services, or other authorities may be warranted.

Marriages and Other Long-Term Relationships

An accurate accounting of all the marital and long-term relationships of the offender is extremely important in sex offender cases. A complete history of all of the offender's significant relationships, including those with both males and females, is important. The circumstances of each relationship, its duration, and outcome should be detailed. Try to obtain a current address and telephone number for each significant person in such relationships. Each relationship should be examined in terms of reasons for entering into the relationship, reasons for any significant separations or conflicts, reasons for the break-up or divorce, and who left whom. The role of each partner in the relationship should be determined. It is useful to know who was the dominant partner, who made what decisions, and what specific responsibilities each partner had in the relationship.

If there were children resulting from any of these relationships, obtain the age, date of birth, current address and nature of any current relationships with each child. Determine if there are court orders related to the support or contact with the child(ren). If there are support obligations, find out if the support is being provided. Try to learn whether there is any history of physical or sexual abuse of any of the children. Include all children who may have been present in the household during the relationship. If the offender maintains contact with children from previous marriages or relationships, address the nature, frequency, and circumstances of those contacts. It may be necessary to regulate and to monitor the contacts to protect the children from risk. If there were any contacts with counselors during any of the relationships, list the dates, periods of counseling, therapists' names and the outcomes of treatment. Where appropriate, obtain written consent from the offender to contact former therapists.

Another important aspect of the offender's significant relationships is an assessment of sexual adjustment in each. Useful information in this area includes frequency of sexual relations, problems or conflicts, dissatisfactions and the extent of communication about sex. Determine the kinds of sexual activity and who initiated such activity. Information about the infidelities of each partner should be included, if applicable.

When possible, contact should be made with those significant persons involved in the offender's current home life. Even if the criminal sexual behavior was not intra-familial, it likely had an impact on the offender's immediate relationships. Determine the current partner's reaction to the sex offense. It is important to learn if the partner was aware of the present and past offenses. If so, try to learn how the partner found out. The partner's reaction to the offender, the victim and to other family members may reveal family dynamics that help to explain the offense. Ask the partner's opinion about why the offense occurred. In the report, comment on the partner's support of the denial patterns of the offender and whether he or she believes the victim's account. Other issues to include are the ability of the partner to be truthful about the offender and the offense, and his/her willingness and ability to participate in treatment programs for the offender.

It is not uncommon for offenders to have entered into relationships with passive partners to gain sexual access to their minor children. Look for a pattern of relationships with women who have children of a particular sex and in a particular age range. Does the offender leave these relationships when the children grow out of his preferred age range?

The reaction of the offender's partner to the crime will reveal a lot about how likely potential victims in the home will be protected from further abuse. In supervision, this information can serve to alert the supervising officer to the offender's potential relapse. The significant others in the offender's life will either support or hinder the work of changing the deviant sexual behavior. Just as in cases of alcoholism, the phenomenon of co-dependent partners and children are a major factor to consider in sex offender cases. Co-dependency (i.e., behaving in ways that enable the acting-out family member to continue doing so) can be a major problem in developing effective supervision strategies.

The special case of intra-family sex offenses. In cases where the father or father figure sexually abuses children within the family, the reaction of the children's mother is very significant. If she knew the sexual abuse was occurring, it is possible that she:

- did nothing to stop it,
- tacitly accepted it,
- participated in making the child(ren) available to the offender, or
- participated in the sexual abuse itself with the primary perpetrator.

If, on the other hand, the mother did not know about the sexual behavior, she may:

- support the child,
- side with the perpetrator (disbelieve the child), or
- refuse to take sides but stop the abuse from continuing.

As can be seen from this analysis, the mother or significant-other adult in the relationship plays an important role in the on-going intra-familial sexual abuse. These considerations argue for thoroughness in gathering marital/partner and family information about the offender.

Other important information to gather in intra-family sex offenses is the offender's relationship with the victim. Signs of favoritism or possessiveness toward the victim should be documented. If there were other children in the family, assess the relationships between the offender and each of those other children. Look for similar patterns of behavior that may suggest other victims or offenses. While investigating the offender's relationship with significant partners (spouse or long-term partners), the officer should assess the appropriateness of current or future residency with the partner.

Justification and basis for special rules. Recommendations for no-contact between the offender and children in the home or other special supervision rules must be provided with a clear rationale. An offender who denies or minimizes the offense and whose significant partner does the same is usually a high risk for probation and reoffending. A home where the family is not cooperative or open with the authorities is also high risk. Homes in which none of the parties — the partner, the offender or the victim — are in treatment are extremely high risk for reoffending. The risk can be lowered by progress in treatment for the offender, the partner, and the victim. As the victim and partner become emotionally stronger, they become better able to notice and to communicate to authorities any deterioration in the offender's behavior. Addtionally, if the investigation does not factually address the rationale for the no-contact provision, judicial or administrative review may not support the officer's recommendations in dispute.

Other Relationships of the Offender

It is common for sex offenders to have very limited outside relationships. Many of the offenders are either socially isolated by their own choice or socially inadequate and unable to establish and maintain friendships and relationships. Others become so compulsive in their deviant sexual behavior that they isolate themselves. Determination of such behavior is important.

Some of the offenders, however, may have friends and frequent companions who either share or, unknowingly, complement the sex offender's deviance. Some seek out companions who share their feelings about women and children. Others seek those who share an interest in pornography or child erotica. Still others try to mask their social inadequacies by joining with younger or considerably older persons. Careful investigation will reveal the presence of any of these factors in the offender's life.

Leisure Activities and Hobbies

The offender's use of leisure time may partially or totally complement his deviant behavior. Ideally, the offender should have leisure activities that offer appropriate tension relief and relaxation. It is important to determine if there are large blocks of unaccounted time that might be used for "cruising" behavior or indulging in fantasies. The officer should ensure that the offender's hobbies do not offer access to potential victims.

Physical Health History

A history of sexually transmitted diseases might reflect patterns of deviant behavior and should be reported. Any physical infirmities or impairments that hinder or affect sexual performance should be included in this part of the report. Any physical disorders or conditions that may be related to disinhibition of aggressive impulses, likewise, should be noted.

Psychological and Emotional History

The presentence investigation report should focus on treatment history involving sexual problems or dysfunctions. Psychological and psychiatric reports should be reviewed for any indications of sexual problems, violent tendencies, and interpersonal difficulties.

Alcohol and Other Drug Usage

Because alcohol and other chemical substances may either enhance or inhibit sexual performance and tend to lessen inhibitions against offending behavior, address the offender's use of alcohol or chemicals and whether that use/abuse contributed to the offender's behavior in the current offense. Many offenders, as a form of denial, will minimize the sexual behavior by blaming the behavior on drugs or alcohol. Determine whether alcohol and other drugs were involved in the offender's pattern of acting out sexually. If they were, then substance abuse treatment is an important part of programming. If substance abuse is an issue for the offender, periods of relapse may constitute times of high risk for sexual relapse.

Prior Criminal and Correctional Records

Special attention should be given to any past adult convictions or juvenile adjudications that were sexually related. The officer should attempt to find and include details from such convictions and adjudications that bear upon the offender's pattern of criminal sexual behavior. Any previous arrests should be reported with special attention given to sexually related issues. If prosecution and/or conviction (adjudication) did not occur, the circumstances and reasons, as available, should be noted. When reviewing previous arrest history, disorderly conduct arrests should be examined for possible sexual connotations. Be alert to burglary convictions that might have actually been sexually motivated crimes. If the offender's pattern of sexual activity in previous arrests and/or convictions involved the use of automobiles for accessing victims, the court may consider revocation or suspension of driving privileges.

Any previous correctional experience should be included: incarcerations, probations or paroles, formal or informal dispositions of arrest, diversionary programs, etc. The offender's performance in diversionary programs and probation should be noted, with special attention given to treatment programs for sexual problems. The offender's comments about the details of past correctional experiences should be included. Previous treatment history often gives an indication of the individual's likely response to treatment in the matter before the court.

Statement of Impact Upon Victim

It is important to obtain information about how the victim has been affected by the offense. The effects may be physical, resulting from injuries received during an offense, from pregnancy or a sexually transmitted disease. Emotional trauma also is likely to be present. Depression, anxiety, fear, anger, and other emotional reactions are common among sex crime victims. Some behavioral reactions, such as disruption in sleep patterns, flashbacks, nightmares, and general changes in social life, also may be present. Any kind of adjustment problems that have developed after the offense should be documented in the report.

Sex crimes often have effects on the victim's social life, including marital problems or relationship difficulties with spouse or boyfriend. When the victim is a child, sometimes problems develop between the parents. The children of an adult victim may experience both psychological and physical reactions. Siblings of victims and members of the extended family may react negatively to the offense and to the victim. Unfortunately, all too frequently family members blame the victim for the offense. Other areas where social problems may develop include friends, companions, co-workers, classmates and in general relations with persons of the opposite sex. Work and school performances may be affected. Statements of impact in these areas should be sought.

When seeking to interview a child victim, the parents of the child will need to be contacted. If they resist subjecting their child to the interview, they should be asked to inform the child of the probation officer's call. Sometimes when parents refuse the officer's request, the child may agree to it. Even if the child initially says "no," interview the parents in their home. Frequently, the child may join in once the interview is underway. When the child appears (even if that is after the interview with the parents is already underway), the probation officer should explain his/her role and purpose. The child can be told that they are being given an opportunity to tell the judge whatever they want.

The victim statement should also spell out the damages that need to be addressed by restitution, including medical costs, lost wages, treatment and other related costs. Wages lost by family members who assist the victim, particularly in the event of a child victim, should not be overlooked. If treatment costs are included, determine the name of the therapist and get the victim's statement of the extent and frequency of the therapy. Obtain a release of information to obtain therapist and other medical information. It is also necessary to determine if other family members may also be receiving treatment and if so, include the details and costs.

When obtaining victim impact statements, tell the victim in advance that the interview will not include questions about the offense itself. Further explain that the victim's statement can help insure that his or her voice is heard in court and that the judge understands how much emotional and physical trauma he or she has undergone.

Victim's Recommendations for Sentencing

In this section of the report, include the recommendations and suggestions made by the victim for an appropriate sentence. When this question is first posed, the response may be very revealing. After some thought the victim is likely to give a more reasoned response. Include both in the report for the court's consideration. When appropriate, determine the victim's suggestions for future needs in relation to the offender. The victim may suggest no-contact provisions or may have suggestions for the reintegration of the offender into the family when intra-family offenses are involved.

Family History

This section of the presentence investigation report should give a clear picture of the offender's family history and background. Accurate information on parents, siblings, step- and half siblings, and extended family are important, because some families have experienced incest or inappropriate sexual behaviors by various members over generations. Taking time to solicit factual data (ages, significance of the relationship to the offender, past convictions, any sexual problems) about significant family members can provide clues about past abuse or sex and gender role models provided the offender as a child. The primary source of family data should be the offender, parents, siblings, and other family members if possible.

After establishing the basic facts about the offender's family, a history of the family's contribution to the offender's values should be included. The focus with sex offenders should be on those family developments that might provide indications about the offender's sexual deviance. Included would be such factors as incest or sexually deviant behavior by other family members, alcoholism, physical abuse, and criminal behavior. Information on how the family discussed or handled sexual issues, sex education, affection, gender roles, and intra-family responsibilities can be very helpful in understanding the deviant orientation of the offender.

Family Attitudes

The reactions of family members to the offender as a person should be addressed in the presentence investigation report, if possible. The family may be willing to confront the offender or may participate in his denial pattern. In addition to giving the officer clues about the offender's support system, the family can supply information that offers additional insight into his deviant sexual problems. Questions might be asked about the offender's overall adjustment and his strengths and weaknesses as a person. Try to determine the patterns of relations with parents or other authority figures in the offender's life. Look for patterns of social isolation or expressions of social inadequacy.

Family members can supply pertinent information about the sexual development of the offender, including any hints of offenses against the offender or by him against others. Family patterns of sex education, dating patterns in adolescence, sex play with siblings or other children, use of pornographic materials and age of opposite sex peers can be gleaned from careful interviews with family members. Family members often will express opinions or provide information about dating, marriage, and parenting behaviors of the offender.

In addition to past history, family members can contribute to knowledge about the offender's past and current criminal behavior. They often will share their opinions of the victim and the responsibility of the offender in the current offense. Recommendations and suggestions for treatment or sentencing should also be solicited from family members and reported.

Religion

Many sex offenders have a strong religious background, and some have repressive sexual attitudes associated with a very rigid and religion-based belief system. Beliefs that are related to the offender's sexual behaviors should be discussed. Other offenders discover religion after being arrested and convicted. This religious conversion may be valid, or it may be a ruse to avoid responsibility, treatment or discussion of sexual behaviors and problems. Others may try to use religion to avoid making changes in deviant fantasy and arousal patterns, avoid court sanctions, or to evade supervisory rules. If there is a doubt about the relationship between the offender's religion and sexual behavior, an individual minister, rabbi, or priest should be consulted.

Sexual History

Some areas of sexual history may be mentioned and reported on in other sections of the presentence investigation report. This section should focus on the offender's self-reports of his/her sexual development, and history (see Chapter 3 and Appendix F). The intent of gathering this information is to discover the offender's level of denial, his deviant fantasy and arousal patterns, and the cognitive distortions supporting the deviance. Most offenders will be reluctant to openly provide the needed information. However, when the offender understands the importance of acknowledging the offense and discussing behaviors, fantasies and arousal patterns and the negative effects of continued denial, accurate sexual histories can sometimes be obtained.

A chronological approach to questioning may make it more comfortable for the offender and the questioner. An appropriate first question is one that deals with the source of sexual information and approximate ages when that information was attained. The circumstances, age of the offender, age and sex of partner, co-participants, and details of the kinds of sexual behavior involved in the first sexual experience is needed. The history of sexual behavior since that first sexual experience should be developed. Include statements of sexual fantasies, patterns of masturbation, orientation toward age and gender, type of sexual activities and characteristics of the sexual partners. How did the offender feel about his/her sexual experiences? Discuss the role of the offender and the partner in terms of passivity or dominance, as well as frequency and duration of sexual experiences. Determine the number of sexual partners and any pattern of casual sex or sex with prostitutes. Ask about patterns of access to sexual partners and preference or dislike for various types of sexual activities. Has the offender ever watched other people engage in sexual behavior? In what context? To what degree and beginning at what age has the offender viewed sexually explicit materials (either pictorial or video)? Ask him to describe those depictions in order to to assess the degree of explicitness. What was his reactions to those materials?

Determine if the offender was the victim of a sexual assault, and, if so, uncover as many details about the offender and each incident of sexual assault as possible. Did the offender witness sex offenses perpetrated by someone else? Did the offender either buy or sell sexual services? Ask for the details of such behavior. A history of sexual preference should be obtained, including statements about sexual attraction to the same or opposite sex and to children. Ask the offender about any doubts he may now have or had in the past about his own sexual capabilities or performance. Histories of sexual dysfunctions are common among sexual offenders, including impotence, premature ejaculation, retarded ejaculation, erectile insufficiencies, and perceived sex organ inadequacies.

Fruitful areas of exploration include questions about the offender's self-perception of his sexual development and his views of himself as a sexual being. Determine if the offender enjoys sex and if he is satisfied or dissatisfied with his sex life. While discussing the likes and dislikes of the offender, it is useful to find out about feelings toward appropriate or inappropriate sexual behavior. Having the offender describe an ideal or perfect sexual relationship may reveal considerable information about feelings and sexuality. Determine if the offender is ashamed of or harbors any guilt feelings about his past sexual behavior and the current sexual offense.

Assessing the Risk

Recommendations in presentence reports are always made with the individual offender in mind. The following are suggested as considerations when determining the appropriate sentencing recommendations and for developing suggested conditions for a supervision court order.

Criteria for determining who represents the greatest risk for reoffending and further harm to the community are listed in Table 6.1. Persons with these characteristics are usually best treated within a secure environment.

The characteristics in Table 6.2 often suggest that the offender is a good risk for probation. Sometimes probation officers and the courts mistakenly use other criteria to determine the appropriateness of incarceration for an offender. Criteria that should *not* be used in deciding to incarcerate the offender include (1) the offender admits the offense; (2) the victim is not a family member; (3) the offender admits previous offenses; (4) the offender admits to other sexually deviant behavior patterns; and (5) he admits to deviant sexual fantasies and planning. The presence of these criteria should not automatically eliminate an offender from consideration for probation.

Special Conditions

The court or parole board may be asked to impose special conditions of probation/parole to prohibit involvement in high risk situations. Examples of special conditions for these offenders might include the following (also see Appendix T):

1. Attend and participate in the sex offender program(s) approved by the Court and the supervising agency in charge of the case.

Table 6.1
Criteria for Incarceration

- Denies the offense
- Uses physical force (especially sadistic behavior)
- Used a weapon
- The offense was a sexual assault
- Previously failed in outpatient treatment
- The offender is a pedophile with a deviant arousal pattern and long history of molesting (fixated pedophile)

Table 6.2
Criteria for Probation

- Admits culpability for the offense
- Admits deviant sexual fantasies and planning the offense
- Has some empathy for the victim
- Shows some distress over his behavior (not just humiliation over being caught)
- Attempted to control the behavior before getting caught

2.   Participate in psychological, psychiatric, and/or psycho-physiological testing and report for clinical polygraph examination(s) as directed by the therapist or supervising officer.

3.   Abide by all rules and conditions of the program and do not leave or withdraw from the program without the permission of the Court, the supervising officer in charge of your case and the program director or his official designate, and

4.   Be responsible for any costs of the program(s).

The conditions of supervision should be stated as specifically as possible to insure that the offender does not find a way to get around the intent of the Court and supervising agency.

Restitution Recommendation

After a review of the victim's impact statement, the officer may choose to make a recommendation for restitution. The victim may have sustained financial loss because of the victimization. That loss may include medical and hospital costs resulting from treatment for physical injuries and similar costs for treatment of psychological trauma. Other considerations in establishing restitution includes loss of work and wages and the cost of treatment for the victim's family in the case of child sexual abuse.

7
Supervising Sex Offenders

The supervision of sex offenders differs from supervision of other types of offenders in several areas. The major difference lies in the area of information. The amount and kind of information needed to supervise a non-sex offender is completely inadequate to supervise a sex offender. Facts about the offense and the deviant behavior of the sex offender are critical for offender supervision. Because denial is almost universally present with the sex offender, officers can expect denial of past and present sexual deviance and denial of deviant arousal fantasies. Because information from the sex offender will probably be difficult to obtain and evaluate, the officer needs to obtain detailed information about the offense from victims or other witnesses. As stated earlier in this book, special care needs to be used in contacting victims in order to avoid adding to the trauma they may have experienced. Information from family members, spouses and significant others will be needed to gain insight into the offender's sexual behaviors and patterns. In evaluating this kind of information the officer should be alert to the possibility that some of these people may also be in denial and colluding with the offender. The supervising officer should gather as much information as soon as possible and base interaction with the sex offender on verified information. Doing so will reduce the time wasted by working through the denials to reach the facts.

Once the facts of the offense are learned, the supervising officer can then begin to learn about the offender's deviant behavior and arousal patterns. Risk and treatment-needs assessments call for this information. Patterns of deviant behavior and arousal patterns, along with other issues in the offender's life, form the basis for risk and needs decisions.

Specific actions are needed to monitor the sex offender's behavior. Because there is such wide variation in sexual arousal patterns and sexual deviance, each sex offender requires specific supervisory actions to inhibit and limit the offender's access to victims or potential victims and to events, places, or situations that might trigger arousal patterns. Intervention at each phase of supervision must be based upon the offender's progress (or lack of it) in managing and controlling his sexual deviance.

Supervisory Tasks

A major task and concern of supervision is to **inhibit the offender's access to situations that create a high risk of reoffending**. Actions must be taken to limit contact with past victims, as well as potential victims. For some offenders, access must be limited to places or environments that trigger fantasies, cognitive distortions or lead to victim grooming. In addition to limiting and inhibiting the offender's access, the supervising officer must help **guide the offender to support groups, treatment programs, or other sources of skill development in sexual and non-sexual problem solving**.

Another critical task in supervising sex offenders is to **developing a routine of reviewing sexual issues** in office reports and home visits. This review should include progress reports from treatment and support groups. The officer needs enough information to evaluate the offender's level of denial (see Chapter 3). It is necessary to review sexual fantasies, masturbatory patterns, and set goals for each report. It is also necessary to review and to reinforce appropriate sexual activity and to review any assignments from the last visit and report. These reports are essential, and sufficient time must be allocated to give them the attention they need.

Legal Issues

Because the court-ordered conditions are likely to be restrictive, legal challenges to the conditions and the officer's supervision are frequently encountered.

Several administrative issues also are involved in the supervision of sex offenders. Because the courts issue new rulings frequently and administrative requirements change, officers should consult their supervisors, and, if necessary, get advice from counsel before acting on any of these issues.

One problem inherent in the supervision of sex offenders is that they require a type of sexual discussion outside the scope of usual social interaction. The type and depth of these sexual discussions create discomfort for many officers. The officer's discomfort with sexual material must be overcome to adequately defend the necessity of the discussions in legal challenges (see discussions of denial and interviewing skills in Chapter 3).

Supervision rules and activities may be challenged by the offender and attorneys in complaints. Offenders and others in their social network may view the necessary sexual discussions as inappropriate and intended for the officer's prurient interest. They may also challenge detailed rules for relapse prevention as punitive and vindictive. Sometimes attempts to accommodate victim/witnesses in violation investigations and revocations may be challenged at every phase of the process. No-contact provisions may be challenged in the convicting court and family courts. The officer needs to be aware of these issues and use strategies to counter them.

The rules of the officer's program for the offender should be based on the factual background of the individual offender, not on strategies generalized from theory. The courts and hearing examiners do not make decisions based upon theoretical treatises. Rather, they will decide issues that are founded in law, administrative rule, or policy and are connected logically and factually to the offender's situation.

The Texas Adult Probation Commission adopted the Strategies for Case Supervision assessment instrument in 1983 as part of its case management system for intensive supervision. This system can be helpful in determining supervision strategies for sex offenders. The purpose of this assessment system is to provide the supervising officer with an efficient and effective case management system. The process is accomplished through the completion of the three system components: an assessment procedure, a supervision planning process, and supervision based upon one of four distinct strategies, depending on individualized case needs. The assessment process consists of inquiries via a semi-structured interview about :

- offender's attitudes toward his/her offense(s)
- offense patterns
- school adjustment
- vocational and residential adjustment
- family attitudes
- interpersonal functioning
- feelings
- plans and problems
- objective background information
- behavioral patterns.

This information is collected to learn the circumstances under which the probationer gets into legal difficulties. After obtaining the above information, the officer assigns the offender to one of four supervision strategies: selective intervention, case-work/control, environmental structuring, and limit setting. Each supervision strategy is described in terms of the probationer's characteristics, goals of supervision, officer-probationer relationship, and supervision techniques (see *Strategies for Case Supervision* manual). The system allows the officer to assume a systematic, proactive role, rather than a trial-and-error, reactive role with the offender.

An area in which discretion and caution is called for is in handling information about the offender's sexual behavior. Officer reports and recordings about the offender's intimate sexual fantasies and arousal patterns can often be kept from disclosure under open records laws.

In probation/parole supervision cases, there is great public interest in encouraging clients to fully disclose information to their supervising officers. If public inspection were granted for information of an intimate personal nature about offenders' lives, these persons would be discouraged from discussing such information with their officers, resulting in greater danger to the public. Therefore, when there is a request for disclosure, the agency must weigh and balance these competing interests, bearing in mind that public policy favors the right of inspection of public records, except where that principal is overridden by a greater public concern for safety served by encouraging disclosure by probation/parole clients.

Such personal and sensitive information should receive special handling and security to protect them from unauthorized viewing. Similarly, sharing information with others, such as employers or spouses, calls for tact and cautious consideration to avoid legal difficulties.

Administrative Issues

Administrative problems often arise and may interfere with effective handling of sex offenders. The biggest is the problem of **workload**. The time needed for proper supervision of sex offenders conflicts with the requirements of a large case load. It takes time to establish and to maintain a meaningful discussion of sexual issues during supervision. In many cases, extra time is needed to monitor residency, employment, and other activities, including confronting the offender's denial. Sex-offender cases also require more collateral effort. Victims, significant others, children, employers, and others in the offender's life require more detailed attention. The officer also needs more time for coordination and consultation with clinicians and others in the community. These activities require more work and more of the officer's time than the cases normally found in the officer's case load.

Officers supervising sex offenders often need their own support system to maintain the proper perspective in managing the offender. The most obvious place for this support is the supervisor. Without the supervisor's support, the officer's plan of supervision will quickly evaporate in the face of the offender's opposition.

Another administrative issue results from the effects of **overcrowded jails and prisons** on sex-offender programs. Disciplinary custody in violations of special rules is an effective tool; however, the tool is sometimes unavailable because of overcrowded county jails. Revocation for failure to follow court or supervision treatment orders establishes a system-wide level of expectation for offenders, whether incarcerated or in the community. Furthermore, current overcrowded conditions often inhibit administrators, courts, and hearing examiners from supporting revocation.

There is no simple solution to these problems. Officers supervising sex offenders need to: have reduced case loads, have technical help available, and be able to bring their problems to supervisors and administrators. Officers can support each other by sharing problems, issues, and solutions.

Court-Impaired Conditions

The court order will be an important starting point for establishing the course of programming for an offender. In supervising the sex offender, special attention should be paid to any special conditions imposed by the court (see Chapter 6). These need to be strictly enforced unless otherwise modified. Any change requires the court's review and authority. The following list of special conditions are frequently imposed on sex offenders.

Jail Sentences

Cases in which probation is seen as appropriate, some jail time also should be imposed as a condition. In child molestation cases, the jail time removes the offender from the home, allows the non-abusing spouse to establish a stronger role in the family, and assures protection for the victim and potential victims. It also serves to confirm that the offender's negative sexual behavior was inappropriate and not the fault of the victim.

Whether the jail time is work-study release or straight time, it is important to let the sex offender know that his activities will be monitored. To actively initiate a program of supervision, the officer should consider requiring verification of employment, hours, attendance, and transportation for work release offenders. Visiting patterns should be reviewed to learn family dynamics and to ensure compliance with no-contact orders. Any participation in support groups in the jail should be documented, and the motivation for participation should be determined. Does the sex offender actually participate in the groups, or is his attendance designed to influence the court or supervising agency to take it easy on him?

Limiting Offender's Contact

Courts will often impose a no-contact order, forbidding or limiting contact between the perpetrator and the victim. This usually means any form of contact (verbal, written, or otherwise). The court may also prohibit contact with specific individuals, categories of individuals, or geographic locations. Sometimes, the court may forbid certain types of employment and activities. The court may order suspension or revocation of driving privileges. The supervising officer needs to review these orders with the offender and to establish how the offender is going to follow them. Because the practical decision may be to remove the offender from the home, some problem-solving may be necessary. Some common problems arising in these discussions include concerns about:

- Ability to finance a separate residence;
- Depression over loss of family contact;
- Defining "supervised" contact with a specific person or category of person (e.g. anyone under the age of 18);
- Finding new employment.

Similarly, the offender's family may experience difficulties with the no-contact provisions. This can even reach the point of undermining the offender's compliance with court orders. The officer will need to help the family understand the importance of changing the pattern of relationships within the family.

Mandatory Treatment

Often, courts will impose evaluation and/or treatment as a condition of supervision. Other times, the offender will have sought treatment and entered therapy before sentencing. The officer needs to obtain a release of information, if needed, and review evaluations and reports. If the offender refuses to provide a release of information, the officer may consider this as a violation of the rules of supervision that require compliance with court orders or cooperation with programming.

The officer will have to determine whether the resources the offender is using satisfy the court's conditions. It is preferable for the court to specifically order the offender to enter into and successfully complete a treatment program approved by the probation department. Otherwise, disputes may arise between the officer and the treatment provider on specific issues, such as the offender's progress, or the pace of family reintegration, or other issues. When there are disputes, the officer should clarify the points of disagreement with the therapist, keep the supervisor informed, and, if resolution does not appear possible, bring the matter before the court for a decision.

If treatment is court-ordered and the offender is not in treatment when the officer receives the case, referral should be made to clinical services or other providers as soon as possible. Programming with support groups such as Parents Anonymous, Sex Addicts Anonymous, Sex and Love Addicts Anonymous, Sexaholics Anonymous, Batterers Anonymous, or other similar programs should not be overlooked as part of a treatment program.

Failure to actively participate in programming can be a risk factor with the offender. Similarly, in examining reintegration into the home, failure of family members to participate in programming can be an indicator of possible continued danger to vulnerable persons in the household. The offender and the family need to know that treatment ordered by the court is an integral part of supervision. The officer must establish that treatment will be taken seriously.

Restitution Requirements

The particular restitution obligations that can arise in sex offender cases may be difficult to determine since treatment on the victim may be ongoing, and there may be no specific amount established at the time of case set-up. The supervising officer should monitor restitution payments to be certain that financial obligations are being met.

Community Service Requirements

Community service assignments need to be evaluated to ensure that contact with potential victims is not facilitated. Placement involving contact with minors is usually the most serious concern. Other supervision requirements are no different from other offenders meeting community service orders.

Court Reviews

A probationer may be returned to court for a review. This hearing may be initiated by the court, the officer, or the offender to review or change conditions. For example, a "no-contact" rule may require endorsement or removal by the court, depending on the circumstances of the case.

Departmental Review

Sometimes the supervising agency may decide to hold an administrative/supervisory hearing as an intermediary step to a show-cause or revocation hearing. With the offender present, his progress or supervisory status is evaluated. Recommendations may be made to the offender about how he can avoid facing a revocation hearing.

Rules of Supervision

When the court does not include specific conditions related to sex-offender issues, the officer may impose special rules of supervision.

Initial Interview of the Sex Offender

In the initial interview of the sex offender, the supervising officer will set the course of supervision. From the beginning, the officer should establish that discussion of sexual problems will be included in the usual report visit with the officer. Reviewing progress in treatment should be a part of reporting. The usual procedures for the home-visit plan, payment of financial obligations, and review of the complaint process should be done during the initial interview.

No-Contact and Residency Rules

In cases of child molestation or intra-family sexual abuse, the offender should be removed from the home and a no-contact provision concerning victims should be in the rules. If the court has not done this, the officer should determine the reason for the omission. If it appears the court would not support a special rule, the supervisor should be informed. The officer may still establish a special rule disallowing any unsupervised contact with minors in the home. Such a rule requires that the non-offending spouse or a competent adult must guarantee supervision, and the children in the home must be made aware of the offender's situation. They would be instructed to inform the officer or other authority if the offender's behavior is out of order. This situation, while uncommon at the beginning of supervision, happens frequently enough to warrant inclusion here. Sometimes when a sex offender is allowed to return home, undue pressure is exerted on the child victim to accommodate the offender back into the family. The victim may then be relegated to a marginal role in the family and again unprotected from revictimization. These issues arise at later stages of re-integration, or when, after a divorce, the offender enters another family, or when the offender tries to have contact with children from previous relationships.

In cases of assaultive behavior with adults, a no-contact provision for the victim may be needed. For those individuals with a history of predatory behavior, structuring contact with potential victims may be in order. For instance, the officer may require the offender to make significant others aware of his past behavior. Sometimes a chaperon contract (see Appendix R) can be arranged between these acquaintances of the offender. A provision of such a contract would be that the offender would disclose to the chaperon when he was going to be around potential victims. An officer may change a no-contact rule to enable beneficial activities, such as victim/perpetrator reconciliation, supervised visitation, family therapy, and time specific and time limited contact. These exceptions suggest that the typical no-contact rule be worded such that no contact with children (victims, etc.) is allowed unless approved in writing by the offender's supervising officer and treatment provider.

In considering potential victims, the officer should keep in mind that some offenders are multiparaphiliacs. Information obtained from the offender's sexual history and plethysmograph findings should be used in deciding whether this is at issue.

In addition to no-contact considerations, the officer should pay careful attention to the offender's residence throughout the course of supervision. Most sexual assault crimes (especially child sexual assaults) happen within a residence. The supervising officer should know the occupants of the offender's residence. Specifically, the officer should be aware of their ages, circumstances, relationship to the offender, and relationship to the supervising adult. Other activities in the home, such as baby sitting, visits by other minor children (relatives or friends) are important pieces of information to determine whether the officer should allow residency or visits to a specific location. Also, the location of the residence and its proximity to past victims or vulnerable persons needs to be assessed.

If a sex offender is being reintegrated with his family, or entering a new family, officer contact with family members is essential. It is important to determine if the minors in the home (either residents or visitors) are capable and willing to bring any improper behavior of the offender to the attention of the supervising adult. Further, the supervising adult should be able to communicate with the officer or other appropriate authorities if the offender's behavior is questionable or deteriorating. Reintegration should be a carefully monitored process, involving consultation with protective service workers, therapists, guardians-ad-litem, and others as appropriate. The offender is not ready to rejoin the family until he has accepted responsibility for his offense and sexual problems and shown remorse and appropriate sensitivity to the victim. Most importantly, the offender should be in a program where "lapses" can be dealt with immediately and firmly.

Other Special Provisions

The supervising officer may impose other special rules based upon factors that contributed to the commission of the sex crime. For example, in the case of a pedophile, prohibitions regarding possession of seduction materials (pornography, video cassettes or toys appealing to children) may be imposed. The individual may be restricted from frequenting parks, school playgrounds, or other high risk geographic locations. "Cruising" is common to compulsive sexual behavior of all types. If the use of a motor vehicle was the means of accessing a victim, or was the actual crime scene, the court may have ordered the offender's driving privileges revoked or suspended. If this was not done, the officer may find it necessary to deny operating privileges or impose certain restrictions, such as permitting driving only to and from work or disallowing driving between certain hours.

The level of control over the offender by special rules should be determined by risk factors. Special rules should be based upon facts about the offender's past sexual behaviors and his arousal patterns, and present behavior. If the offender continues to deny and minimize, to blame the victim, and is not progressing in treatment, then strict rules of supervision are required. Special rules should be based upon facts about the offender's past sexual behaviors and his arousal patterns, and pre-

sent behavior. Restrictions on the use of alcoholic beverages, controlled substances, places of employment, or driving may be appropriate.

Offenders who are required to undergo treatment might
also be required either by the court or the agency to submit to
periodic polygraph and/or plethysmograph (or comparable
arousal measurement in women) examinations at the direction of
the treatment provider and supervising officer in order to determine if the conditions of supervision are being complied with.

It is useful to have the court order the offender to pay for all
of the costs associated with his treatment (initial diagnostic evaluation, psychophysiological assessments, individual and group
treatment) as a condition of probation.

Other rules to consider include curfew conditions and activity logs, and living conditions (e.g., proximity to schools, playgrounds, parks, etc.).

Sometimes it is better to include many of the above special
conditions in a treatment contract and then to use the polygraph
to confirm compliance. Supervising officers should have copies of
such treatment contracts.

Employment Status

Meaningful supervision requires that the officer be aware of
the offender's employment status and any changes in employment. The officer must use discretion concerning employer contact. A sex offender might not tell his employer of his conviction
and supervision status, because he feels the information could
jeopardize his employability. In some areas of the country sex offenders are required to tell their employers that they have been
convicted of a sex crime. The probation officer checks with the
employer to verify that the offender has done so. Sometimes the
officer may determine that direct contact with the employer is
unnecessary. Employment might be verified by a check stub.

Some offenders may obtain certain employment positions to avoid being available to participate in treatment. The officer can help in setting priorities when conflicts between employment and treatment occur.

Abrupt employment changes may be indicative of an increased "risk" situation. Therefore, such a pattern may merit investigation. When a sex offender's conviction or prior record relates to the conditions of employment, the officer should restrict the offender's employment. If this is not feasible, the employer must be notified of the offender's supervision status. A pedophile should not be allowed to be employed as a daycare worker, a maintenance person in a daycare center, a baby sitter or permitted any employment that places him in contact with children. The supervising officer must be concerned about access to potential victims. The officer should know enough about employment positions to be able to assess whether an offender would exploit a position of authority for sexual reasons. The officer may terminate an offender's employment situation with cause. For the officer's protection, his or her supervisor should be consulted before such action is taken.

Home Visits

The importance of home visits in sex-offender cases is obvious. An officer should be observant regarding the personal belongings of the offender that might be used to seduce potential victims. A pedophile's residence, for example, may manifest age inappropriate features that alert the officer to possible problems. The presence of toys, dolls, comic books, games, model planes or boats in the residence of a child molester where there are no children clearly suggests the possibility of continued offending. Because most pedophiles have limited age preferences, the inappropriate materials usually will be suitable for that age range. For instance, if the offender has a history of offending against teenagers, the materials in his home may include youth oriented items, such as rock-star posters, games, and records. Another signal to the supervising officer is the presence of pornography in the home. Excessive fascination with camera equipment or photographs of children throughout the home may be another indicator of risk.

Travel Permits

In issuing travel permits, the officer should be alert to possible contact with victims or potential victims. The officer should review the proposed travel to insure that risk issues have been addressed and that a plan for handling possible problems has been developed.

Notification of Law Enforcement

Notification of law enforcement regarding movement of sex offenders is an important part of community protection. The supervising officer should establish a working relationship with the police officers assigned to the sex crimes unit in the area and routinely inform them of new cases coming into the area via transfer, interstate compact, or release from jail or prison. Similarly, in cases where reintegration into the home is occurring, protective services should be informed. The officer might also keep a photograph of each sex offender on his/her caseload to assist the police when they come asking about the location of a particular offender.

Intrastate and Interstate Transfer and Direct Assignment Cases

When receiving transfer or direct assignments from other geographic areas, it is important to review the sex offender's file for completeness of information about the offender's criminal sexual behavior and patterns of sexual arousal. The receiving officer also needs information concerning the offender's level of denial and response to treatment. If the individual has been sent with reporting instructions, it is preferable to confirm the information with the sending officer/state.

The same principles for determining risk used in the presentence and residency and employment sections discussed earlier are applicable to transfer and direct assignment cases. If the offender is moving with his family or into a new family, the family dynamics need to be considered for possible risk. An interstate transfer request may be rejected if the transfer involves inordinate risk of reoffending. If it appears that the offender intends to transfer in order to avoid participation in a treatment program or to escape the accountability of the officer's supervision practices, the case should be reviewed with the supervisor to determine whether the transfer should be rejected.

Sometimes a transfer may occur before an evaluation has been completed in the county or state of jurisdiction. Such an evaluation may be requested of that jurisdiction or a modification of the conditions of supervision in the court of jurisdiction may be requested to include mandatory participation in the assessment and subsequent treatment program. If a transfer is received on an offender who is not required to participate in therapy, the supervising agency should seek to modify the conditions of supervision in the court of original jurisdiction.

Violations and Revocation Issues

With sex offenders, the supervising officer can expect the same type of violations seen in other cases: domestic violence, drug and alcohol related problems, driving infractions, problems with reporting, and more serious criminal behavior. When the violation relates to the sexual problems of the offender, special attention should be given to the risk of reoffending. In domestic violence, the offender may be continuing a pattern of sexualizing anger. In child sexual abusers, the violation may indicate intimidation of the mother-figure of the household and possible risk to minors living there.

Problems with drinking or drug abuse may be an indicator of loss of control and may warrant aggressive action to secure outpatient, or, with continued violations, inpatient programming. Non-reporting or absconding might stem from the offender's fear of facing his sexual problems.

Some violations directly relate to supervision. Some of the more common ones include violations of no-contact orders/rules, failure to participate and progress in treatment, failure to follow through on relapse prevention strategies or on treatment assignments. Violations must be handled in accordance with standard procedures. Violations often provide an opportunity for the offender to learn about the seriousness of his sexual problems. Often, the violations represent turning points in the supervision. So revocation should not be the first choice for violations unless they involve new offenses. Counseling, amended rules, disciplinary custody, placement in residential facilities, and other alternatives should be considered before revocation. The decision to revoke the privileges of treatment needs to be made in accordance with standard policies and procedures.

New Allegations of Sexual Offenses

If the officer believes that the offender has been involved in a new sexual offense, the offender should be placed in custody, pending completion of the investigation. If the offender is not available for custody, an apprehension warrant should be issued, and law enforcement informed. Whether or not the offender is detained, a "no-contact" rule should be imposed to insure that there is no attempt to intimidate or coerce the victim. If the offender's family becomes involved in intimidation, it may be necessary to alert police and the district attorney.

Signed statements from the victim and any witnesses should be secured, preferably notarized. Every effort should be made to avoid multiple interviews with any victims, especially child victims. Working with law enforcement, protective services, examining medical professionals, and the district attorney is recommended. Not only can these other professionals be resources for testimony in hearings, but they also may help in interviewing the child. The officer should review any reports from the above agencies to become familiar with the incident. Releases for medical records or treatment reports need to be signed by the adult or by a parent of a minor victim. If the testimony from a a victim or a witness looks as though it might present problems, the officer's supervisor should be involved. If appropriate, the officer should help victims find treatment resources.

Revocation Procedures

In writing allegations for revocation, try to use only allegations admitted by the offender, or ones that can be supported by victims or witnesses under cross-examination. Optimally, admissions by the offender should be in writing, with as much clarity as possible on details. Avoid using names of crimes, such as "rape," or "sexual assault." Instead, describe specific behaviors, specific dates, and specific locations. Separate different behaviors into different allegations in case any are rejected because of technicalities. The officer should be aware that polygraph records concerning new offenses are not admissible in court, but polygraph results can be used when an offender is found to have violated the conditions of his probation/parole.

Choose witnesses who can support the allegation for the revocation action. If police, protective services, or other professionals were involved in the investigation of the allegation, they should also be subpoenaed. Prepare the witness(es) for the hearing. It is helpful to review the testimony in detail before the hearing. Reviewing the testimony provides an opportunity to assess the victim's attitude toward the offender and the alleged offense.

Before a child is called to testify, describe the physical environment and acquaint the young victim or witness with the hearing procedure. Try to show children where the offender will be seated. If the child knows in advance that the offender will be there, the hearing itself may be less traumatic, and the child may have fewer problems testifying. Have a supportive person, such as a child's mother, a relative, therapist, or victim/witness professional accompany the child and sit next to the child throughout the proceeding.

If intimidation of a child victim is a major problem, previous arrangements for testimony behind a screen or a one-way mirror might be attempted. Prior consultation with the officer's supervisor and legal counsel are essential. When questioning a child witness, use language the child can understand. It may be necessary to establish the meaning of words used by a witness. Frequently, if the witness lacks verbal skills, the use of anatomically correct dolls may be used to demonstrate the activity which occurred.

If the allegation was not reported immediately by the victim, review the reasons for the delay. If the child's story changed in the investigative phase, account for this during the questioning. If victims or witnesses are ambivalent in their feelings toward the offender, review these feelings in the hearing. Raising these issues first and in a straight-forward manner, reduces the risk of the victim's position being distorted on cross-examination. If you suspect the victim or the witness will tell a different version at the hearing, you may still be able to prove the violation by introducing prior statements from the victim or witness into the record.

Revocation hearings for sex offenders do not differ significantly from those for other offenders. The officer can expect to see similar problems. A witness may change testimony, be intimidated by the presence of the offender, or refuse to testify. Some witnesses may perjure themselves while others add embellishments to their testimony that lack veracity.

After the testimony, provide support to the child. Be alert to any possible emotional problems or fear of retaliation the victim may be experiencing. If appropriate, involve staff as an additional resource when the child appears to be unusually upset. If there is a pending criminal complaint against the offender, the district attorney's office should be informed of the status of revocation proceedings. The offender may request to delay the revocation hearing until after a criminal trial.

Preparole Plans

Residency. The inmate's proposed residence should be verified through a home visit. Contact should be made with the adult head of the household to assess the environment in which the inmate expects to live. Occupants of the household need to be aware of the inmate's history of sexually deviant behavior. Part of determining the adequacy of the residence is the officer's assessment of the ability of potential victims to be protected and to protect themselves. If the living arrangement is not acceptable because of an unreasonable risk of recidivism, it may be rejected. Justification should be documented and an alternative plan proposed by the officer.

By law, victims must be informed about the parole eligibility of the offender. They can also submit written opinions about parole decisions. Victims may contact the officer for information or clarification about the inmate's parole status. These contacts often provide a sense of community attitudes toward the offender. Sex offenders often are stigmatized by the objectionable crime committed. If a pervasive sentiment of animosity toward the offender is found in the community, release to an alternative community may be more realistic.

For those sex offenders participating in treatment in the institution, a release plan providing for continuity should be implemented. If a halfway house placement is being considered, the officer may attach a program statement to the preparole investigation. Intention to use community resources to aid the inmate's transition from the institution to the community should be indicated in the parole plan, with a listing of the resources available. Officers are encouraged to comment regarding the suitability of an inmate's parole plan. A professional analysis of the inmate's risk and needs at the time of consideration for parole should be offered.

Discharge

Interested parties may be informed that the Department of Corrections or Criminal Justice no longer has control over the offender after discharge. Law enforcement officials should be informed if a "high risk offender" is discharged, especially if the offender is discharged directly from a correctional institution and is expected to move into the area.

Victims of Sex Offenses

An understanding of the offender's victims and their victimization is important in supervision. Unfortunately, the officer's main source of information about the victim is usually the offender, because the officer spends proportionately more time with the offender's analysis and version of the offense than with that of the victim. Furthermore, the officer is flooded with the perpetrator's distroted thinking about victims with every contact.

Sexual deviance is part of an arousal pattern ingrained in the thought processes and fantasy life of many sex offenders. Included in the offender's arousal pattern are distorted images of victims. The offender usually overcomes feelings of shame and repulsion by justifying his behavior (offender distortions to justify various crimes were discussed in Chapter 3). The most effective justifications are cognitive distortions of the victim's situation.

The officer may unwittingly agree with some of these distortions. For example, an officer may accept an offender's rationalization that adult-child sexual behavior is not necessarily "all that bad" if the child initiates the activity, is older than some arbitrary age, and accepted some form of reward for the sexual activity.

Changing the offender's attitude toward victims is part of the program to reduce the risk of repeat offending. The officer's behavior and attitudes model a stance toward victims and victimization for the offender. For these reasons the officer as a role model can have significant implications for the offender's views of victims. It is important to spend some time thinking about sexual assault victims and the dynamics operating in the officer's contacts with them. The discussion below is far too brief and lacking in detail to be adequate. For more detailed information concerning this topic, officers are directed to the bibliography. Officers should also develop a close working relationship with the victim/witness programs in their area. These programs can provide invaluable information, material and support for those supervising sex offenders.

In any sexual assault case or in any criminal case, the offer of treatment to victims and their families, is strongly recommended. Generally, officers should learn the dynamics of victimization to more professionally respond to the victim's needs. The most difficult victim issues are: inability to provide enough time for the victim's needs; inability to provide more protection for victims because of the offender's rights; difficulties interviewing young victims; and difficulties with co-dependent victims and/or their families.

The Effects of Sexual Victimization

Victims of any crime report the following experiences. They feel a vague sense of guilt for having been chosen, and they wonder if they gave out some type of signal that attracted the offender to them. These feelings lead to a sense of complicity with the act. They feel guilty that they did not take more action to prevent or stop the victimization. They feel shame and embarrassment that friends and acquaintances are aware of the crime. Victims often feel they are "marked" by the crime. They feel violated and invaded. They feel vulnerable because they could not take care of themselves and because they feel that perhaps the victimization will happen again. Because they are usually seduced or manipulated into the behavior, the belief is reinforced. The offender's denial and blaming add to these feelings.

Child Victims

When children are sexually victimized, their sexual thoughts, feelings, and actions, already a source of embarrassment, are brought to the light of day and shared with a host of others. These others may include parents, family members, schoolmates, school officials, protective service workers, law enforcement officers, court personnel, victim advocates, medical staff, attorneys, judges, and probation and parole staff. The feelings of guilt are often made worse by the reactions of others who place the blame on the child or who react as though the child is somehow "dirty" or contaminated. Some treat the child victim of sex crimes almost as though the child had a contagious disease that would spread like an epidemic if the child comes into contact with others.

The reaction of the child victim is further complicated when there is a relationship with the offender (relative, neighbor, friend or role model — teacher, pastor, coach, adult leader). Often, the victim may have had a very positive relationship with the offender up to the point of victimization. Offenders who victimize children often are very good at gaining the trust and the affection of the child before beginning the sexual activity with the child. The victim then has to deal with strong feeling of ambivalence. The decision to report, prosecute, and testify in adversarial proceedings is extremely difficult for the victim, especially when the offender mounts an aggressive defense against the charges.

Sexual Abuse in the Family

The child victim's position is again further complicated in cases of intra-family child sexual abuse. The child has been victimized by someone who is supposed to be trusted and loved. That trust has been destroyed and that love distorted into sexual activities. The child has been warned not to tell anyone and that to tell will bring disaster to the family. The relationships with all family members is disrupted by the victim's decision to bring the criminal sexual behavior to light. The mother feels betrayed by the husband and perhaps by the victim as well. The victim feels responsibile for the sexual behavior, the offender's incarceration, and the negative effects on all involved.

The sexual abuse may have already isolated the victim in the family system. This isolation may be increased when the offense is reported. The offender is often required to leave the home, or the children in the home may be removed and placed in alternate care situations. Siblings and other relatives suffer embarrassment because of the public nature of prosecution. Siblings and others blame the victim for the disruptions that occur. It is not uncommon for the mother and the rest of the family to turn against the victim and support the offender. Family members may blame the child victim for their mother's depression after the father was asked to leave the home. Faced with these kinds of pressure, some children recant their allegations.

For these reasons, reporting victimization usually calls for an act of courage by the child. That act may be brought on by desperation, but it requires a great deal of courage on the part of the child.

Because of the family dynamics operating in intra-family child sexual abuse, several intervention strategies are suggested. The perpetrator, not the victim, should be removed from the home. If the mother and/or the rest of the family are so hostile that protection cannot be afforded the victim, an appropriate petition should be filed and treatment ordered for the child and family. A guardian-ad-litem can be appointed for the victim. If alternate placement for the child is necessary, the perpetrator should stay outside the home until placement and a course of treatment is finished.

In cases where the family remains intact, the treatment should focus on strengthening the relationship between the victim and the non-offending parent while the offender is out of the home. When this is accomplished, family therapy prepares the individual family members for the return and reintegration of the perpetrator into the home. Part of this process should include family therapy that focuses on repairing the relationship between the perpetrator and the victim. Until this reintegration is accomplished the offender should not be allowed contact with any of the children (especially if a plethysmographic evaluation has not been conducted). Each step of reintegration should be accompanied by therapy assignments for all participants. The assignments are designed to insure the safety of the victim, the reinforcement of gains made in the therapy, and the restructuring of the family's alliances. In cases of divorce or separation, child protection and the offender relationship with a non-offending partner still needs attention should the offender decide to enter another family. Also, visitation arrangements with the offender's children from previous marriages or relationships also need officer monitoring.

During preparole planning, some spouses may recant their earlier support for the child's version of the offense in order to allow the offender to return home immediately upon release. Caution should be exercised in accepting such a statement in order to protect the victim and not collude with the offender.

Adult Victims of Sex Crimes

Victims commonly report long-term loss of trust in their judgment about other people. If the assault was perpetrated by a stranger, victims will question how they contributed to vulnerability. "Why did I get on the elevator with that person?" If the assault was by someone known to the victim, victims are commonly plagued with doubts about their ability to establish relationships. These feelings of inadequacy usually have lasting implications for the victim.

Adult victims also experience shame and disruption in their immediate relationships. Spouses or close friends may withdraw from the victim because they have irrational doubts about complicity in the sexual behavior. The assault may severely disrupt the victim's sex life, causing alienation of the individual's partner. The embarrassment of revealing intimate sexual details in the legal proceedings, knowing that one's associates know about a sexual victimization, all have a traumatizing effect on the adult, similar to that felt by a child.

Conclusion

This book has incorporated an up-to-date summary of present thinking and knowledge about sex offenders, effective treatment strategies, and principles of supervision. The reader should realize that there are still wide gaps in our knowledge. Clearly, not every sex offender who is referred for treatment is going to profit from it. In fact, many offenders appear to be particularly intractable and cannot be safely re-integrated into society. Theoretical perspectives of the causes and maintenance of sexual offending are only emerging, and, at present the theories that are available represent a diversity of views. While it is apparent that careful evaluations of treatment are only in their infancy, such appraisals do indicate that effective treatment programs for some offenders are possible. Continued research is needed with long-term follow-up studies on large samples of treated offenders.

Although there is reason for optimism regarding the likely outcome of future efforts to deal with sex offenders, it is important to underline that treatment is offered to only a small proportion of sex offenders who need it. Even in areas where treatment programs are in place, many programs are biased toward selecting the offenders thought most likely to succeed. Identifying the characteristics of those persons who respond most effectively to any treatment program should not encourage the establishment of exclusionary criteria, but rather should encourage the development of innovative and alternative programs for those for whom available treatments presently fail.

Persons working in supervisory and/or treatment positions with sex offenders need to appreciate the evolving nature of this field. In order to be effective in supervision and treatment efforts, officers need to stay current in the field. Continuing education should be a regular feature of the professional development of all providers in this area.

Appendix A
Selected Bibliography

Able, G., J. Becker, M. Mittleman, J. Cunningham-Rathner, J. Rouleau, and W. Murphy. "Self-Reported Sex Crimes of Nonincarcerated Paraphiliacs," *Journal of Interpersonal Violence*, 2, no. 1, (1987): 3-25.

Abel, G., M. Mittelman, J. Becker. "Sexual Offenders: Results of Assessment and Recommendations for Treatment." In *Clinical Criminology. The Assessment and Treatment of Criminal Behavior*, M. H. Ben-Aron, S. Huckle, C. Webster (eds.) . Toronto: M and M Graphic Ltd., (1985): 191-205.

Able, G., J. Becker, M. Mittleman, and J. Becker. "Sexual Offenders: Results of Assessment and Recommendations for Treatment." In *Clinical Criminology. The Assessment and Treatment of Criminal Behavior*, M. H. Ben-Aron, S. Huckle, C. Webster (eds.). Toronto: M and M Graphic Ltd., 191-205, 1985.

Abrams, S., and B. Abrams. *Polygraph Testing of the Pedophile*. Portland: Gwinner Press, 1993.

Alexander, M. *Sex Offender Treatment: A Response to the Furby et al., 1989, Quasi Meta-Analysis II.* Paper presented at the Annual Meeting of the Association of the Treatment of Sexual Abusers, San Francisco, Calif.

Andrews, D., and J. Bonta. *The Psychology of Criminal Conduct.* Cincinnati: Anderson Publishing Company, 1994.

Barabaree, H. E., W. L. Marshall, E. Yates, and L. Lightfoot. "Alcohol Intoxication and Deviant Sexual Arousal in Male Social Drinkers," *Behaviour Research and Therapy*, 21, (1983): 365-73.

Barabaree, H. E., M. C. Seto, R. C. Serin, N. L. Amos, and D. L. Preston. "Comparisons Between Sexual and Nonsexual Rapist Subtypes: Sexual Arousal to Rape, Offense Precursors, and Offense Characteristics," *Criminal Justice Behavior*, 21, no. 1, (1994): 95-113.

Bartlow, D. "The Treatment of Sexual Deviation: Towards a Comprehensive Behavioral Approach." In *Handbook of Behavioral Assessment*, K. Calhoun, H. Adams, and K. Mitchell (eds.), New York: Wiley, 1974.

Becker, J., and J. Hunter Jr. "Understanding and Treating Child Adolescent Sexual Offenders." In Ollendick, T., and R. Prinz (eds.) *Advances in Clinical Child Psychology*, 19, New York: Plenum Press, 1997.

Berlin, F. "Sex Offenders: A Biomedical Perspective." In J. Grier and I. Stuart (eds.) *Sexual Aggression: Current Perspectives on Treatment*, I, New York: Van Nostrand Reinhold, 1982.

British Committee on Obscenity and Film Censorship. *Report.* London: Her Majesty's Stationery Office, 1979.

Campbell, J. *Assessing Dangerousness.* Thousand Oaks, Calif.: Safe Publications, 1995.

Carish, M., and D. Adkerson. *Adult Sexual Offender Assessment Packet.* Brandon, Vt.: Safer Society Press, 1995.

Chaffin, M. "Assessment and Treatment of Child Sexual Abusers," *Journal of Interpersonal Violence*, 9, no. 2, (1994): 224-37.

Check, J. V., D. Perlman, and N. M. Malamuth. "Loneliness and Aggressive Behavior," *Journal of Social and Personal Relationships*, 2, 243-52.

Christie, M. M., W. L. Marshall, and R. D. Lanthier. *A Descriptive Study of Incarcerated Rapists and Pedophiles.* Report to the Solicitor General of Canada, Ottawa, 1979.

Cumming, G., and M. Buell. *Supervision of the Sex Offender.* Brandon, Vt.: Safer Society Press, 1997.

Dietz, P. E. "Sex Offenses: Behavioral Aspects." In *Encyclopedia of Crime and Justice*, S. H. Kadish et al. New York: Free Press, 1983.

Donnelly, S., and R. Lieb. *Community Notification: A Survey of Law Enforcement.* Olympia, Wash.: Washington State Institute for Public Policy.

Donnerstein, E. "Pornography and Violence Against Women: Experimental Studies, " *Annals of the New York Academy of Science,* 347, (1980): 277-78.

Edmunds, S. *Impact: Working with Sexual Abusers.* Brandon, Vt.: Safer Society Press, 1996.

Elliott, M. (ed.) *Female Sexual Abuse of Children.* New York: Guilford Press, 1993.

Emerick, R. *A Comparison of Female Preference Child Molesters: Adolescent or Adult Onset.* Paper presented at the Annual Conference of the Association for the Treatment of Sexual Abusers, Boston, Mass.

English, K., S. Pullen, and L. Jones (eds.). *Managing Adult Sex Offenders: A Containment Approach.* Lexington, Ky.: American Probation and Parole Association, 1996.

Finkelhor, D. *Child Sexual Abuse: New Theory and Research.* New York: Free Press, 1984.

Fisher, W. A., and D. Byrne. "Individual Differences in Affective and Behavioral Responses to an Erotic Film," *Journal of Applied Social Psychology,* 8, (1978): 355-65.

Freeman-Longo, R., and F. H. Knopp. "State of the Art Sex Offender Treatment: Outcome and Issues," *Annals of Sex Research,* 5, (1992): 141-60.

Furby, L., M. Weinrott, and D. Blackshaw. "Sex Offender Recidivism: A Review," *Psychological Bulletin,* 105, (1989): 3-30.

Gray, A., and R. Wallace. *Adolescent Sexual Offender Assessment Packet.* Brandon, Vt.: Safer Society Press, 1992.

Gray, S. H. "Exposure to Pornography and Aggression toward Women: The Case of the Angry Male," *Social Problems,* 29, 387-98.

Greenfield, L. A. *Sex Offenses and Offenders, Summary.* Washington, D.C.: U.S. Department of Justice, 1997.

Groth, A. N. "Guidelines for the Assessment and Management of the Offender." In *Sexual Assault of Children and Adolescents,* A. W. Burgess, et al. Lexington, Mass.: Lexington Books, 1978.

Groth A. N. *Men Who Rape: The Psychology of the Offender.* New York: Plenum Press, 1979.

Haaven, J. R. Little, and D. Petre-Miller. *Treating Intellectually Disabled Sex Offenders.* Orwell, Vt.: Safer Society Press, 1990.

Hanson, R. K., and M. T. Bussiere. "Sex Offender Risk Predictors: A Summary of Research Results," *Forum on Corrections Research,* 8, no. 2, (1996): 10-12.

Hare, R. *Without Conscience: The Disturbing World of the Psychopaths Among Us.* New York: Pocket Books, 1993.

Hunter, M. *Child Survivors and Perpetrators of Sexual Abuse.* Thousand Oaks, Calif.: Safe Publications, 1995.

Johnson, K. M. *If You Are Raped,* 2nd ed. Holmes Beach, Fla.: Learning Publications, 1998.

Knight, R. A. and R. A. Prentky. "Classifying Sexual Offenders: The Development and Corroboration of Taxonomic Models." In *Handbook of Sexual Assault: Issues, Theories, and Treatment of the Offender,* W. L. Marshall, D. R. Laws, and H. E. Barbaree (eds.). New York: Plenum Press, 1990.

Knight, R. A. and R. A. Prentky. "The Development, Reliability, and Validity of an Inventory for the Multidimensional Assessment of Sex and Aggression," *Criminal Justice and Behavior,* 21, no. 1, (1994): 72-93.

Knopp, F. *Retraining Adult Sex Offenders: Methods and Models.* Syracuse, New York: Safety Society Press, 1984.

Laws, D. R. (ed.). *Relapse Prevention with Sex Offenders.* New York: Guilford Press, 1989.

Laws, D. R., and W. L. Marshall. "A Conditioning Theory of the Etiology and Maintenance of Deviant Sexual Preference and Behavior." In W. L. Marshall, D. R. Laws, and H. E. Barbaree (eds.), *Handbook of Sexual Assault: Issues, Theories, and Treatment of the Offender.* New York: Plenum Press, 1990.

Malamuth, N. M., and J. V. Check. "The Effects of Mass Media Exposure on Acceptance of Violence Against Women: A Field Experiment," *Journal of Research in Personality,* 156, (1981): 436-46.

Malamuth, N. M., and J. V. Check. "Rape Proclivity Among Males," *Journal of Social Issues,* 37, (1981): 138-57.

Malamuth, N. M., S. Haber, and S. Feshbach. "Testing Hypotheses Regarding Rape: Exposure to Sexual Violence, Sex Differences, and 'Normality' of Rape," *Journal of Research in Personality,* 14, (1980): 121-37.

Maletzky, B., and K. McGovern. *Treating the Sexual Offenders.* Thousand Oaks, Calif.: Sage Publications, 1989.

Marquis, J., D. Day, C. Nelson, and M. West. "Findings and Recommendations from California's Experimental Treatment Program." In G. Hall, R. Hirschman, J. Graham, and M. Zaragoza (eds.), *Sexual Aggression: Issues in Etiology, Assessment, and Treatment.* Washington, D.C.: Taylor and Francis, 1993.

Marshall, W. L. "The Use of Explicit Sexual Stimuli by Rapists, Child Molesters, and Nonoffender Males," *Journal of Sex Research,* 25, (1988): 267-88.

Marshall, W. L., and H. E. Barbaree. "An Integrated Theory of the Etiology of Sexual Offending." In *Handbook of Sexual Assault: Issues, Theories, and Treatment of the Offender,* W. L. Marshall, D. R. Laws, and H. E. Barbaree (eds.), New York: Plenum Press, 1990.

Marshall, W. L., R. Jones, T. Ward, P. Johnston, and H. Barbaree. "Treatment Outcome with Sex Offenders," *Clinical Psychology Review*, 1991.

Marshall, W. L., and W. Pithers. "A Reconsideration of Treatment Outcome with Sexual Offenders," *Criminal Justice and Behavior*, 21, no. 1, (1994).

Matthews, R., J. Hunter Jr., and J. Vuz. "Juvenile Female Sexual Offenders: Clinical Characteristics and Treatment Issues," *Sexual Abuse: A Journal of Research and Treatment*, 9, no. 3, (1997).

Matthews, R., J. Matthews, and K. Speltz. *Female Sexual Offenders*. New York: Safer Society Press, 1990.

Mayer, Adele. *Women Sex Offenders*. Holmes Beach, Fla.: Learning Publications, 1992.

Mendel, M. The *Male Survivor*. Thousand Oaks, Calif.: Sage Publications, 1995.

Miletski, H. *Mother-Son Incest: The Unthinkable Broken Taboo*. Brandon, Vt.: Safer Society Press, 1995.

Murphy, W. "Assessment and Modification of Cognitive Distortions in Sex Offenders." In *Handbook of Sexual Assault: Issues, Theories, and Treatment of the Offender*, W. L. Marshall, D. R. Laws, and H. E. Barbaree (eds.), New York: Plenum Press, 1990.

Murphy, W., E. Coleman, R. A. Prentky. "Treatment and Evaluation Issues with the Mentally Retarded Sex Offender." In *The Sexual Aggressor: Current Perspectives on Treatment*, J. Greer and I. Stuart (eds.) New York: Van Nostrand, 1983.

O'Connell, M., E. Leberg, and C. Donaldson. *Working with Sex Offenders*. Thousand Oaks, Calif.: Sage Publications, 1990.

Quinsey, V., and C. Earls. The Modification of Sexual Preferences. In In *Handbook of Sexual Assault: Issues, Theories, and*

Treatment of the Offender, W. L. Marshall, D. R. Laws, and H. E. Barbaree (eds.), New York: Plenum Press, 1990.

Pithers, W. D. "Treatment of Rapists: Reinterpretation of Early Outcome Data and Exploratory Constructs to Enhance Therapeutic Efficacy." In G. C. N. Hall, R. Hirschman, J. R. Graham, and M. S. Zaragoza (eds.), *Sexual Aggression: Issues in Etiology, Assessment, and Treatment.* Washington, D.C.: Taylor and Francis, 1993.

Prentky, R., and A. Burgess. "Rehabilitation of Child Molesters: A Cost-Benefit Analysis." In A. W. Burgess (ed.), *Child Trauma: Issues and Research,* New York: Garland Press (1992): 417-42.

Prentky, R., and S. Edmunds (eds.). *Assessing Sexual Abuse.* Brandon, Brandon, Vt.: Safer Society Press, 1997.

Prentky, R., and R. Knight, A. Lee, and D. Cerce. "Predictive Validity of Lifestyle Impulsivity for Rapists," *Criminal Justice and Behavior,* 22, no. 2, (1995): 106-28.

Quinsey, V., G. Harris, M. Rice, and M. LaLumiere. "Predicting Sexual Offenses." In J. Campbell (ed.), *Assessing Dangerousness: Violence by Sexual Offenders, Batterers, and Child Abusers.* Thousand Oaks, Calif.: Sage Publications, 1995.

Quinsey, V., and M. Lalumiere. Assessment of Sexual Offenders Against Children. Thousand Oaks, Calif.: Sage Publications, 1995.

Rada, R. T., D. R. Laws, and R. Kellner. "Plasma Testosterone Levels in the Rapist," *Psychosomatic Medicine,* 38, (1976): 257-68.

Rosencrans, B. *The Last Secret: Daughters Sexually Abused by Mothers.* Brandon, Vt.: Safer Society Press, 1997.

Salter, A. *Treatment Skills for Professional Working with Sex Offenders.* National Institute of Corrections. Washington, D.C.: U.S. Department of Justice, 1989.

Schmauk, F. J. "Punishment, Arousal, and Avoidance Learning in Sociopaths," *Journal of Abnormal Psychology*, 76, (1970): 325-35.

Stewart, A. J., and M. Sokol. *Male and Female Conceptions of Rape*. Paper presented at meeting of the Eastern Psychological Association, Boston.

Sourcebook of Criminal Justice Statistics 1995. Washington, D.C.: U.S. Department of Justice and Bureau of Justice Statistics, 1996.

Stermac, L., and Z. Segal. *Cognitive Assessment of Child Molesters*. Paper presented at the 21st annual convention of the Association for the Advancement of Behavior Therapy, Boston, 1987.

Thomas, S., and R. Lieb. *Sex Offender Registration: A Review of State Laws*. Olympia, Wash.: Washington State Institute for Public Policy, 1995.

Turner, M., and T. Turner. *Female Adolescent Sexual Abusers*. Brandon, Vt.: Safer Society Press, 1994.

United States Commission on Obscenity and Pornography. *The Report of the U.S. Commission on Obscenity and Pornography*. New York: Random House, 1970.

Wahler, R. G. "Oppositional Children: A Quest for Parental Reinforcement Control." *Journal of Applied Behavior Analysis*, 2, (1969): 159-70.

Yates, E., H. E. Barbaree, and W. L. Marshall. "Anger and Deviant Sexual Arousal," *Behavior Therapy*, 15, (1984): 287-94.

Yochelson, S. and S. Samenow. *The Criminal Personality. Vol. 2: The Change Process*. New York: Jason Aronson, 1977.

Appendix B
Reading List

Adams, C., and J. Fay. *No More Secrets*. San Luis Obispo, Calif.: Impact Publishers, 1981.

Allred, T., and G. Burns. (eds.). *Stop! Just for Kids*. Brandon, Vt.: The Safer Society Press, 1997.

Armstrong, L. *Kiss Daddy Goodnight: A Speakout on Incest*. New York: Pocket Books, 1978.

Bach, G. R., and H. Goldberg. *Creative Aggression: The Art of Assertive Living*. New York: Avon, 1975.

Bass, E., and L. Davis. *The Courage to Heal: A Guide for Women Survivors of Child Sexual Abuse*. New York: Harper and Row, 1988.

Bays, L., R. Freeman-Longo, and D. D. Hildebran. *How Can I Stop? Breaking My Deviant Cycle: A Guided Workbook for Clients in Treatment*. Brandon, Vt.: The Safer Society Press, 1990.

Bays, Laren, and Robert Freeman-Longo. *Why Did I Do It Again? Understanding My Cycle of Problem Behaviors: A Guided Workbook for Clients in Treatment*. Brandon, Vt.: The Safer Society Press, 1990.

Bear, E., and P. Dimock. *Adults Molested as Children*. Brandon, VT: The Safer Society Press, 1988.

Berman, S. *The Six Demons of Love: Men's Fears of Intimacy*. New York: McGraw Hill Books, 1984.

Bloomfield, H. H. *Making Peace with Your Parents*. New York Ballantine Books, 1983.

Brady, K. *Father's Days: A True Story of Incest*. New York: Dell, 1979.

Calhoun, L. G., J. Selby, and H. E. King. *Dealing with Crisis: A Guide to Critical Life Problems.* Englewood Cliffs, N.J.: Prentice Hall, 1976.

Carnes, P. *Contrary to Love.* Minneapolis: CompCare Publications, 1989.

Chiauzzi, E., and S. Liljegren. *Staying Straight: A Relapse Prevention Workbook for Young People.* Holmes Beach, Fla.: Learning Publications, 1991 .

Collins, G. R. *Overcoming Anxiety.* Wheaton, Ill.: Key Publishers, 1973.

Comfort, A. *The Joy of Sex.* New York: Fireside, 1972.

Conway, J. *Men in Mid-Life Crisis.* Elgin, Ill.: David C. Cook Publishing, 1983.

Cullen, M., and R. Freeman-Longo. *Men and Anger.* Brandon, Vt.: The Safer Society Press. 1996.

Davis, L. *The Courage to Heal Workbook: For Women and Men Survivors of Child Sexual Abuse..* New York: Harper and Row, 1990.

Davis, M., E. Eshelman, and M. McKay. *The Relaxation and Stress Reduction Workbook.* Richmond, Calif.: New Harbinger Publications, 1981.

Dowling, C. *The Cinderella Complex.* New York: Pocket Books, 1982.

Freeman-Longo, R., L. Bays, and E. Bear. *Empathy and Compassionate Action.* Brandon, Vt.: The Safer Society Press, 1996.

Freeman-Longo, Robert, and Laren Bays. *Who Am I and Why Am I in Treatment?: A Guided Workbook for Clients in Evaluation and Beginning Treatment.* Brandon, VT: The Safer Society Press, 1988.

James, M. *The O.K. Boss.* New York: Bantam, 1976.

Johnson, S. *Man-to-Man*. Brandon, Vt.: The Safer Society Press. 1992.

Kahn, Timothy J. *Pathways: A Guided Workbook for Youth Beginning Treatment*. Brandon, Vt.: The Safer Society Press, 1990.

Kiley, D. *The Peter Pan Syndrome*. New York: Dodd, Mead, 1983.

Kiley, D. *The Wendy Dilemma: When Women Stop Mothering Their Men*. New York: Avon, 1984.

Knopp, F. H. *When Your Wife Says No*. Brandon, Vt.: The Safer Society Press, 1994.

Lew. M. *Victims No Longer: Men Recovering from Incest and Other Sexual Child Abuse*. New York: Harper and Row, 1990.

Madox, L. *Anger*. New York: Charles Scribner, 1972.

McCabe, T. R. *Victims No More*. Center City, Minn.: Hazelton, 1978.

Mornell, P. *Passover Men, Wild Women*. New York: Ballantine, 1980.

Naifeh, S., and G. W. Smith. *Why Can't Men Open Up?* New York: Warner Books, 1984.

Pithers, W., A. Gray, C. Cunningham, and S. Lane. *From Trauma to Understanding*. Brandon, Vt.: The Safer Society Press, 1993.

Powell, J. *The Secret of Staying in Love*. Niles, Ill.: Argus Communications, 1974.

Rubin, T. I. *The Angry Book*. New York: Collier Books, 1978.

Ruitenbeek, H. *The New Group Therapies Book*. New York: Avon, 1970.

Russianoff, P. *Why Do You Think I am Nothing Without A Man?* New York: Bantam, 1982.

Samenov, S. E. *Inside the Criminal Mind*. New York: Time Books/New York Times Book Co., 1964.

Selye, H. *Stress Without Distress*. New York: Lippincott, 1974.

Smith, G. W. *Couple Therapy*. New York: Collier Books, 1973.

Stearns, A. K. *Living Through Personal Crisis*. New York: Ballantine, 1984.

Steen, C. *The Relapse Prevention Workbook for Youth in Treatment*. Brandon, Vt.: The Safer Society Press, 1993.

Appendix C
Acknowledgment of
Nonconfidentiality and Waiver

I, _____, have been informed and ac-
knowledge that my rights to confidentiality are limited, insofar as
my treatment at _____ is concerned. I
have also been informed and acknowledge that whatever I tell an
interviewer or counselor during treatment is not privileged or
private. If any such rights of confidentiality, privilege or privacy
exist or, subsequent to execution of this waiver, are held to exist
by statute or rule of law, I hereby waive any and all such rights
with respect to communications about me between my therapist
and the person(s) listed below.

Name_____

Position_____

Address_____

Name_____

Address_____

Address_____

I understand that the sex offense of which I have been convicted is a criminal offense with serious consequences to the victim and the community, and I hereby allow any therapist to
report to the agency responsible for my supervision any occurrence or potential occurrence of a sexual offense on my part, regardless of how the therapist gains knowledge of such occurrence
or potential occurrence. The purpose of my participation in
_____ treatment program is to control my

sexual behavior, and I wish to be held fully accountable for such behavior.

Signature of Client _____

Date _____

Witness _____

Date _____

Appendix D
Release of Information

I, _____, authorize the _____
Texas Department of Criminal Justice — Community
Supervision and Corrections Division/Pardons and Paroles
Division and _____ to exchange oral and
written diagnostic, referral, and treatment information about me.

Information to be released:

❑ Name

❑ Diagnostic information/institutional adjustment

❑ Referral information

❑ Attendance data

❑ Clinical progress notes

❑ Education/treatment termination information

❑ Medical history and exam reports

❑ Other (specify) _____

This authorization for release of information pertains to
criminal justice purposes. The specific charge(s) involved is(are):

_____

This authorization remains in effect and may not be revoked until court requirements in connection with the above
specified charge(s) have been fulfilled.

_____

_____   _____

Signature of Offender   Signature of Witness

Date _____

Appendix E
Interview Questions

Offender's Honesty

1. Tell me what offenses you committed and why?
2. How do you think the victim(s) of your offenses were affected by what you did to them?
3. How excited were you before, during and after you committed your crimes?
4. How angry are you at the victim for reporting you?
5. What were you not honest about when you talked to the police?
6. What did you not tell the police about your crimes?
7. Who have you lied to about this problem?
8. How do you feel about coming here for an interview about your offenses?
9. How much of a problem do you think you have with being honest?
10. What have you gotten out of being secretive and and dishonest?
11. What are the problems you are having in your life now?

General Sex-Offender Questions

1. When did you become a sex offender?
2. How have you arranged your life to make it easier to offend?
3. How do you feel about yourself before, during and after offending?
4. What thoughts and feelings occur to you while thinking of your history of specific sexual behaviors?
5. How did you learn your sexual behaviors?

6. What kinds of things are going on in you or in your life just before you decide to commit a sex offense?

7. What makes you continue to engage in your sex crimes? What are you getting out of them?

8. How have your sexual deviations changed over time?

9. How often have you peeped in windows?

10. How often have you exposed yourself?

11. How often have you made obscene phone calls?

12. How often have you rubbed up against another person in public for sexual purposes?

13. How have you tried to stop your deviant behavior?

14. How have your sexual problems affected other areas of your life (e.g., school or work effectiveness, social life, family interaction, health, finances, sexual intimacy)?

15. What is missing in your life now?

16. Discuss your relationships with important adults (male and female) in your life.

Sexual Assault

1. What time of day did you commit or attempt to commit your offenses?

2. Describe in detail the place(s) where you committed the offenses.

3. Why did you choose those places? Do you always choose the same kind of place or does it vary?

4. How did you get to the place(s) where you committed your crimes?

5. Who was with you or nearby when you committed your offenses? Did they see what you were doing? Are you usually alone when you offend or with others? Who are the others and what is your relationship to them?

6. For how long have you known your victim(s)?

7. How old were you when this happened? How old was your victim at the time?

8. When did you first start thinking about this type of offense? When did you first start fantasizing about this particular victim?

9. How did you plan on keeping your crime a secret and avoid getting caught?

10. How did you approach the victim? What did you say? How did you gain her/his cooperation?

11. How many times have you broken into a house/store and stolen something? Have you ever broken into a house/store when you knew someone was there? Were they asleep? What else did you want to do?

12. How many times have you committed a sexual assault at the same time you were committing another crime?

13. What exactly did you do to your victim(s)? How did you touch or hold the victim? Where did you touch them?

14. How did you perform oral sex on the victim? How did the victim react?

15. How did you perform intercourse (i.e., vaginally or rectally) with the victim? Were you able to get an erection? Were you able to keep your erection? Did you ejaculate?

16. What else did you do to your victim(s)? How did you get the victim to perform oral sex on you? Did you hold, restrain, or threaten him/her? Did you ejaculate during oral sex?

17. Did you make the victim undress or did you undress him/her? Did you tear his/her clothes?

18. Did you insert any objects into the victim at any time? Did you have the object with you before the offense?

19. What did you say to the victim(s) during the offense? What did you say after the offense was over?

20. How did you get the victim(s) to go along with the offense? What kinds of threats did you use?

21. What types of weapons have you used during your offenses? Did you tell the victim you had a weapon even if you did not? Did you touch the victim with the weapon? Did you put the weapon anywhere inside the victim? How sexually exciting was this to you?

22. What did you tell the victim you would do if he/ she told anyone about what you did?

23. How many times have you sexually assaulted this person?

24. Describe in detail any physical hitting, beating kicking, burning, cutting, etc. during the offense. What were you thinking or feeling at the time you were doing these things? How sexually aroused were you by these things?

25. Did you tie the victim up? Did you blindfold the victim? Why and how?

26. Did you urinate or defecate on the victim?

27. Did you kill, attempt to kill, or think about killing any of your victims? What did (would) you do with the body? Did you have any sexual contact with the victim after that person's death?

28. What did you want to do to the victim that you did not do? Why didn't you do that?

29. Tell me what your rape fantasies are like?

30. How do you feel about women/girls in general? Do you have any problems getting along with certain women/girls? Do you ever think women act as if they are better than you or able to control you somehow?

31. Were you drinking alcohol or using drugs at any time prior to or during the offenses? What and how much did you take?

32. When you left the scene of the offense, how did you leave your victim?

Child Molestation

1. What have been the ages of the children you have molested? What have been their relationships to you?

2. What has been the sex of the children you have molested? Does the sex of the child make any difference to you?

3. Have the children you molested been prepubertal or postpubertal (sexually mature)? Does it make any difference to you if the child you sexually abuse is sexually mature? Why or why not?

4. What time(s) of the day did you commit your offenses? Where did they take place? How did you get there?

5. How many different children have you molested for which you never got caught?

6. How old were you when you first started sexually abusing children?

7. How much time out of a day or week do you spend thinking about offending before you commit the offense? How much thinking do you do before an offense about particular victims?

8. How do you go about getting yourself into a position or situation so you can molest a child?

9. What determines which child you choose to molest?

10. What did you do specifically to your victims? Did you remove their clothes or have them do it? How did you fondle him/her? Exactly where did you fondle the child and how? How did you perform oral sex of your victim? Did you

have vaginal intercourse with the child? Why or why not? Did you have anal intercourse with the child? Why or why not?

11. Did you masturbate in front of the child? Did you have the child masturbate you? Did you ejaculate?

12. Did you have the child perform oral sex on you? How did you get them to agree to do it? Did you ejaculate?

13. Did you ever have your victims perform sex act on other children while you watched? If so what kinds of things did you have them do? How did the children react to that?

14. How often did you do these things with the same child? How often did you do them with different children?

15. Did you take pictures of or videotape the children you molested? Where are those pictures? What do you do with the pictures you take? What were the children doing when you photographed them?

16. How many children have you attempted to molest but gave up for some reason? Why did you give up?

17. How did you get the child to go along with your requests? What did the child do to attempt to verbally or physically stop you? What did you do to counter those things? What did the child say to you during the offense? What did you say to the child during the offense? Did you ever give the child money, presents, or special privileges to keep quiet about what you did or to gain their cooperation?

18. What did you do to physically force or restrain the child? Did you use a weapon of any kind?

19. How do you make sure the sexual abuse would remain a secret?

20. Who else was present during your offenses? Who else knew what you were doing to the children? Did anyone bring the

child(ren) to you or instruct them to go to you knowing what you intended to do to them?

21. Were you ever caught sexually abusing a child? Who caught you and what did they see and do?

22. How many separate sexual incidents did you have with each of your victims?

23. Tell me about your fantasies about sexually abusing children. Do the fantasies involve male or female children? What age range?

24. What pornography did you use to get the child's interest or curiosity? What pornography do you use to get sexually aroused and to begin thinking about molesting kids?

25. What kind of games did you play with your victim(s)?

26. How do you feel before, during and after your sexual offenses?

27. What are the kinds of things that are going on in your life just prior to your crimes? What led up to your crimes?

28. Were you drinking alcohol or using drugs during any of these offenses? What and how much were you using? Did you give alcohol or drugs to your victims during the molestation?

Exhibitionism

1. Tell me specifically how you exposed yourself? What did you want it to look like you were doing? What type of vehicle did you use? Where did you you sit or lie down? Were the windows/doors open or closed?

2. How were you feeling just prior to, during, and after the offense?

3. How long did you follow or watch your victim(s) before you exposed yourself?

4. How much time during the day or week do you think about exposing yourself?

5. Where do you usually expose yourself? How did you pick this place? How many times have you exposed yourself there? How many different locations have you used to expose yourself? Describe those locations.

6. What time of the day or night do these offenses usually take place? Why then? What day of the week is it when you usually expose yourself? Why then?

7. What are the ages of your victim(s)? Are they usually men or women, boys or girls?

8. How do you get the attention of your victims?

9. How well did you know your victim(s)? Where did you first meet or see them?

10. What exactly do you do during the offenses? Do you masturbate during or after the offenses? Do you usually ejaculate? When? When you expose yourself, do you usually take all of your clothes off or only some of them. Do you usually have an erection by the time a victim notices you?

11. How much actual contact did you have with your victim(s) during the offense(s)?

12. What do you say to the victim during the offense? What have they said to you when they have seen you exposing yourself?

13. Approximately, how many times have you exposed yourself?

14. How do your victims react? How do you want them to react? What do you do when the victim reacts? What is the most arousing reaction you have gotten? What were you doing at the time and what did you do when she/he reacted like that? How did it make you feel? What is the worst reaction you have gotten? What were you doing at the time and

what did you do when she/he reacted like that? How did it make you feel?

15. How old were you when you first exposed yourself? Describe where you were, what you did and what happened.

16. Have you ever exposed yourself out of a window of a building? Have you ever exposed yourself in any other situation? If so, describe it.

17. Have you ever left the bathroom door or other door slightly open while you were dressing, urinating, bathing, masturbating, or just lying naked hoping that someone would see you?

18. Have you ever exposed yourself to the same victim more than once?

19. Why do you think you expose yourself?

20. Were you drinking alcohol or using drugs just prior to or during any of these offenses? What and how much?

Voyeurism

1. How and where did you look in windows? What and who were you trying to see? Did you know them?

2. How old were the persons you hoped you would see or did see?

3. What did/would you do if they saw you?

4. How much have you thought about going inside and having sex with someone inside? How many of those thoughts involved situations in which you force the person to have sex with you if they don't go along?

5. How many times have you broken into the house or building where you had seen someone? What were your intentions? What did you take? What else did you do before you left? Did you break, vandalize, or deface anything?

6. How many times have you returned to the same place to look in windows or break in?

7. How many times have you ever broken into a house/apartment and waited for someone to come home? Who were you waiting for? Why?

8. Do you use binoculars or a telescope to spy or your victims?

9. How are you feeling at the time you look in windows? How often do you masturbate while looking? Do you ejaculate? How do you feel afterwards?

10. How old were you when you first started thinking about looking in windows?

11. How much time of the day or week do you spend thinking about this or getting into situations where you could do it?

Obscene Phone Calls

1. From what location do you make these calls?

2. Tell me specifically what you say? How do you keep the person on the line?

3. How did you find the numbers of the people you called? How did you decide who to call? Who were you hoping would answer the phone?

4. How many of the people you have called do you know personally or know of?

5. What exactly were you doing during the call? Do you masturbate during or after the calls?

6. How many times have you done this in the past?

7. How many of your calls do you make alone? How many times have there been other people with you? Who introduced you to the idea of making calls?

8. What were you feeling and thinking just prior to making the call and during the call? How did you feel after making the call?

9. What reaction did you hope for from the persons you were calling? What in fact was their reaction most of the time?

10. How old were you when you made your first obscene phone call?

11. How did you get caught?

12. How much time out of a day or week do you spend thinking about this or getting into situations where you could do it?

Other Sexual Aggression

1. How often have you shoplifted or stolen things? What would you do with the things you took? Have you ever stolen women's underwear? How and where? What do you do with the underwear?

2. How many times have you touched another person's body in a sexual way when he/she was not aware of what you were doing? How many times have you tried?

Appendix F
Sexual History

Prior to the interview, review any and all previous evaluations, reports, etc., with particular attention to victim reports and police reports. The sexual history is probably best taken after the rest of the social history is completed. This allows for some degree of comfort to develop between the officer and the offender. While taking the history, keep the emphasis on relationships with people, rather than on sex per se. This will put the client at ease and produce more information. It is important that the officer retain a nonjudgmental attitude and avoid indicating shock or surprise. When obtaining information, maintain skepticism about the frequency data obtained from the offender.

Life History

Early and Middle Childhood (under 12 years of age). This period extends up to the time of puberty.

1. Familial attitudes toward sex and affection; include parental models of affection and parental concerns about the behavior of their children.

2. Early sex information
   - how information was acquired and at what age the offender figured out what sex was "all about"
   - preparation for menstruation and nocturnal emissions and who provided the information.

3. Early sexual experiences
   - sexual activity with parents, siblings, same-sex and opposite-sex peers and other adults; get specific details.

Adolescence (12 to 18 years of age). Sexual activity tends to "set" into fairly stable patterns, and early experiences provide the foundation upon which these patterns elaborate.

1. Age at which dating began
    - frequency of dating
    - number of people dated
    - pattern of dating one person exclusively or simultaneous dates.

2. Age of first climax
    - masturbation history (how often, when, where, with whom, feelings about
    - frequency and associated fantasies; sex and fantasy aids (pictures, videos, movies, books).

3. Age of first sexual experience with another person (coitus, petting or other)
    - sex and relative age of partner
    - setting; frequency
    - feelings about the experience.

4. Other sexual experiences with others
    - number of sex partners
    - sex and age of other persons
    - kinds of sexual activity
    - frequency of sexual activity
    - use of coercion or force
    - pattern of accessing partners
    - preferred/disliked sexual behaviors
    - settings (money exchanged)
    - relationships to current sexual fantasies
    - feelings about the experiences.

5. Other significant influences
    - birth control methods

- pregnancies
- venereal diseases
- use of prostitutes.

Early Adulthood Years (18 to marriage). Review information listed above in the 12 to 18 years of age section.

The Married Years. Focus on sexual adjustment with spouse. Break information down into chronological periods: first six months, next 18 months, and each ensuing five-year period. In each time period, inquire about changes in or frequency of sexual activity.

1. Frequency of masturbation
2. Frequency of intercourse
3. Perceived sexual pleasure from offender
4. Perceived sexual pleasure from spouse
5. Description of any problems encountered: orgasmic incompetence or concerns about frequency of sex
6. Range of activities, experiences
7. Extra-marital activities
8. Known or suspected infidelity on part of spouse
9. Birth control methods
10. Experience with same-sex erotic contact.

Victimization

1. Experience as a victim of rape or molestation
2. Trauma from observing sexual interaction and victimization of others.

Stress Management

1. Kinds of stress common to offender's experience
2. Methods of handling stress.

Sexual Values

1. "Good/bad" sex, homosexuality, masturbation, extramarital sex, etc.

Sexual Offenses

1. Offender's description of the offense
    - assessment of reliability
    - acknowledgement of responsibility
    - empathy for victim; antecedent thoughts, feelings and behaviors
    - reaction to apprehension
    - reason for the offense
    - actions before the offense occurred
    - feelings (anger, depression, anxiety, boredom)
    - activities (pornography, cruising, planning, isolating victim, interpersonal conflict)
    - use of substances before the crime
    - thoughts and fantasies before, during and after the crime
    - relationship with the victim
    - previous inappropriate sexual activity with the victim.

2. The first deviant act; get specific details;
    - age of offender
    - age of victim
    - sex of victim
    - method used to gain access to victim
    - method used to gain compliance from victim
    - what else was happening in offender's life at the time
    - what led the offender to engage in the act

- how he felt during and after and what were the consequences

3. Subsequent deviant sexual acts; summarize offender's sex history by projecting frequency and number of victims over the person's life.

   - number of acts
   - kinds of acts
   - number of victims
   - age of victims
   - sex of victims
   - fantasies that preceded the behaviors
   - methods used to gain access to victims
   - methods used to gain compliance of victims
   - how offender felt before, during and after each offense
   - consequences after each offense

4. High risk situations

5. Triggers of deviant fantasies

   - mood swings
   - interpersonal conflicts

6. Deviant sexual fantasies

7. Cognitive distortions

8. Overview of present life situation relationships with significant others and children; employment; friends; avocations religion; sexual adjustment.

Following the completion of the interview, the offender should be given a general explanation of what your recommendations will be.

Appendix G
Psychosexual Assessment

An important component of the presentence investigation is the psychosexual assessment of the offender. Generally, the assessment shall include a clinical interview, personality tests, a battery of pencil-and-paper inventories, and the penile plethysmograph.

1. Review of relevant law enforcement reports.

2. The victim's statement of the offense.

3. The statements or evaluations of those who are close to and/or assisting the victim (i.e., family, counselor, teacher, etc.).

4. The offender's statement of the offense(s).

5. A standard intelligence test.

6. Minnesota Multiphasic Personality Inventory.

7. Clinical interview including, but not limited to, the offender's social history, sexual history.

8. Interview of spouse or significant other.

9. Review of past evaluation(s) and treatment history.

10. Paper-and-pencil inventories, selected as appropriate:

    a. Abel and Becker Card Sort of Sexual Fantasies

    b. Abel and Becker Cognitions Scale

    c. Attitudes Toward Women

    d. Burt Rape Myth Acceptance Scale

    e. Buss-Durkee Hostility Inventory

    f. Family Adaptability and Cohesion Evaluation Scale

    g. Fear of Evaluation Scale

    h. Interpersonal Reactivity Index

    i. Michigan Alcohol Screening Test

      j.   Multiphasic Sex Inventory

      k.   Nowicki-Strickland Internal/External Control Scale

      l.   Social Avoidance and Distress Scale

      m. Speilberger State-Trait Anger Scale

      n.   Wilson Sexual Fantasy Questionnaire

      o.   Crowne-Marlowe Scale of Social Desirability

11. Penile Plethysmograph

12. Evaluation of offense pattern, including the amount of violence, amount of risk taken, whether the offense appears predatory, explosive or opportunistic, and the use of disinhibitors.

13. Situational considerations:

      a.   access to victim(s)

      b.   how much is at stake

      c.   the legal hold over the offender

      d.   the number of natural monitors in the offender's life

      e.   the social and sexual outlets available to the offender

      f.   the attitudes of people around the offender.

14. Impressions and prognosis.

15. Recommendations

      a.   appropriateness of outpatient treatment

      b.   risk to the community

      c.   treatment needs and planned treatment modalities

      d.   planned monitoring techniques

      e.   planned restrictions on offender's behavior

      f.   required conditions of treatment.

Appendix H
Consent to Pychophysiological Assessment of Sexual Interests

A sexual-arousal assessment is done to help your therapist learn more about your sexual urges. During this assessment you will be questioned about your history, with specific details asked about your sexual behavior.

Your sexual interests will be measured by recording your penile-erection response while you look at sexually explicit slides and/or listen to audio tapes. This sexual material is very graphic and will include nondeviant sexual behavior and deviant sexual behavior relating to your problems. While observing or listening to these sexual materials, your erection will be measured by a small penile transducer, an apparatus you will place around your penis in a private room. This device is thoroughly cleaned with an antiseptic to kill germs.

There are certain risks involved in this procedure. You may feel anxious, uncomfortable, depressed, or angry. You may worry so much about how you will do that you may have problems getting an erection during or after the assessment. If you have any of these problems, the examiner or your therapist will help you if you ask.

The benefits of this assessment are that it will show which (if any) treatment is needed because of your sexual interests and arousal patterns. The results of this assessment will be communicated to you by your therapist. The results also will be forwarded to your supervising officer.

Alternative means of evaluation include interviews and psychological testing without the direct measurement of your erection response. You may wish to choose that form of evaluation if you have excessive concerns about measurement of your erection response during this assessment.

You may voluntarily withdraw your consent for this procedure at any time during any stage of this assessment.

Your signature below indicates that you have read and understood all of the above and voluntarily submit to this assessment.

_____

Subject signature   Date

_____

Evaluator signature

_____

Witness signature

Appendix I
Consent to Behavioral Treatment

You are asked to participate in treatment specifically designed to reduce your sexual arousal to deviant themes and/or increase your sexual arousal to nondeviant themes. During treatment you may be shown explicit sexual slides, asked to listen to explicit sexual tapes or asked to verbalize or imagine explicit sexual behavior. This sexual material will depict deviant sexual behavior as well as nondeviant sexual behavior relating to your problems.

Your treatment could include *aversive conditioning,* which is a procedure that pairs deviant sexual material with aversive elements. Aversive elements include noxious scenes and noxious odors (ammonia, etc.). Noxious odors are administered by means of a squeeze bulb that passes the odor to your nose. The use of aversive elements may result in increased anxiety and/or nausea. This anxiety may carry over to outside the treatment room and cause you to have fears about your sexual performance, and you may develop difficulty getting an erection.

The benefits of the treatment are that it will decrease deviant sexual arousal and assist in overcoming your habitual pattern of sexual deviancy.

Alternative means of treatment include group therapy and individual therapy without aversive conditioning. You may wish to choose this means of treatment if you have excessive concerns about the aversive conditioning process.

At any stage of treatment you may withdraw your consent to this treatment.

By signing this statement you are giving your voluntary consent to participate in all of the above, and indicating that you have read and understood the nature of this treatment.

Subject signature   Date

Therapist signature

Witness signature

Appendix J
Consent to Psychopharmacological Treatment

Psychopharmacological treatment, such as the administration of Depo-Provera, can be useful in reducing your sexual arousal to and interest in deviant sexual themes. You have already participated in treatment designed to reduce your deviant sexual arousal, but those methods have not been very successful. It is because you still have significant deviant arousal that this form of medical treatment is recommended for you.

Depo-Provera is administered on a weekly basis by injection. Serum testosterone (sex hormone levels in the blood) will be monitored before and periodically during this treatment process. Plethysmographic assessment may also be conducted.

The dosage of Depo-Provera will be sufficient to reduce your testosterone level to prepubertal levels. During this treatment you will be participating in behavioral therapies, including aversive counter-conditioning. Once your deviant sexual arousal is reduced to an insignificant level, your weekly dosages of medication will be reduced monthly until you are no longer taking it.

The benefits of treatment are that it may reduce your deviant sexual arousal and assist in overcoming your habitual pattern of sexual deviancy.

The potential side effects resulting from use of Depo-Provera include: weight gain, increased need for sleep, cold sweats, hot flashes, testicles may decrease in size, hyperglycemia, hypertension, nightmares, elevated blood glucose, muscular pain, labored or difficult breathing, decreased sperm count, abnormal sperm, nervousness, and upset stomach. You may also have difficulties obtaining erections and the overall desire to sexualize or fantasize may decrease. These side effects are temporary while receiving this medication and are reversible.

At any stage of treatment you may withdraw your consent for psychopharmacological treatment by submitting your withdrawal in writing to the prescribing physician.

In signing this you are indicating that you have read and understood the above and do voluntarily participate in this treatment.

_____

Subject signature   Date

_____

Therapist signature

_____

Witness signature

Appendix K
Group Guidelines

1. The purpose of group therapy is to encourage personal growth and self-awareness so that each member will learn more appropriate ways of coping with his life. Preventing reoffending is the main goal.

2. Members of the therapy group should expect confrontation, and sometimes painful work, on past experiences that may have contributed to the decision to offend, and that continue to affect each participant today. Expect support too. Group therapy provides each member with an opportunity to share feelings and thoughts with others who have had some of the same experiences.

3. The group will discuss both feelings and behaviors in the past and present. Some of the issues that will be addressed include the following:
   - Sexuality
   - Intimacy
   - Nonsexual expressions of affection
   - Sex-role stereotyping
   - Male-female sexual needs
   - Self-destructive thoughts and behaviors
   - Fantasizing
   - Obsessive thoughts/compulsive behaviors
   - Chemical abuse
   - Suicide and suicidal equivalents
   - Addictive behaviors (e.g., work, gambling, etc.)
   - Social isolation
   - Alienation

- Avoidance and withdrawal
- Responsibility
- Defensive reactions (e.g., denial, minimization, rationalization, projection, displacement)
- Ownership of behaviors, thoughts, feelings
- Exploitive behaviors
- Objectification of others (i.e., lack of empathy)
- Manipulation, lying, "conning"
- Parenting and family needs
- Communication (e.g., attending behaviors, assertiveness, "I" messages, honesty)
- Maturity
- Family roles and role reversals
- Family and sexual history
- Unmet needs for nurturance
- Childhood trauma (i.e., physical, emotional and sexual abuse)
- Affective responses
- Anger (e.g., sublimation, compensation, passive-aggressiveness, suppression, repression)
- Guilt, remorse (or absence of), shame
- Impulsivity (i.e., lack of control)
- Stress management
- Relaxation skills
- Behavioral management of stress
- Awareness of triggering events
- Problem-solving skills development
- Conflict management

- Environmental manipulation
- Communication
- Self-esteem
- Peer support
- Assertiveness training

4. Regardless of whether your attendance at group therapy is mandatory or voluntary, you will be asked to leave the group if you refuse to deal with your issues, if you continue to abuse drugs or alcohol, or if you miss three group sessions without telephoning to explain your absence. Probation and parole officers are notified of any unexplained absences.

5. Confidentiality is respected at all times, except regarding re-molestation. You should expect that if sexual reoffending recurs, it will be reported to the authorities. If you are fantasizing about reoffending, you should share those feelings in the group. Feelings are not criminal offenses — behaviors are. The group serves to help you deal with fantasies and feelings so that you do not act out in ways that are harmful to others.

6. The group is open-ended, so that members join as the need arises. You should expect to be in group therapy for at least one year. After about six months, you should expect to assume more responsibility in group and model appropriate behaviors for new members.

7. Group leadership is shared. You are expected to take an active role in helping create a meaningful group experience for everyone.

8. Members with drug and alcohol problems are expected to refrain from use and to attend a program, such as AA, that is designed specifically to address chemical abuse.

9. The emotional tone of the group is accepting and nonjudgmental. The group is a safe place where you can be yourself, deal with issues, relieve stress, and receive both support and advice. Group members are encouraged to share telephone numbers and contact one another between meetings. Also, members are asked to read recommended books and handouts and to share insights and learnings with others in the group.

_____

Member's signature   Date

_____

Therapist's signature

_____

Witness signature

Appendix L
Self-Evaluation of Behavior in Group Therapy

Circle the number that represents your behavior in group.

	Not at all		Some-times		Often	Score
1. Expresses ideas freely and openly	1	2	3	4	5	_____
2. Listens attentively to others	1	2	3	4	5	_____
3. Gives suggestions/opinions	1	2	3	4	5	_____
4. Asks for suggestions and opinions from others	1	2	3	4	5	_____
5. Accepts feedback well	1	2	3	4	5	_____
6. Focuses on major issues (past and present)	1	2	3	4	5	_____
7. Demonstrates a desire to change	1	2	3	4	5	_____
8. Confronts others when necessary	1	2	3	4	5	_____
9. Acts as a team member (neither domineering nor withdrawing)	1	2	3	4	5	_____
10. Helps others disclose	1	2	3	4	5	_____
11. Adheres to group norms and helps set standards	1	2	3	4	5	_____
			Total			_____

Comments:

Feel free to share your results with others during the feedback sessions.

_____

Member signature   Date

Appendix M
Values Questionnaire

A. (This questionnaire elicits information about impulse/anger control, sexuality, problem-solving skills, moral development, use of defenses, stress management, and social isolation.)

Answer each of the following questions in two or three brief sentences.

1. How often do you feel that your boss has been unfair to you? What do you usually do about this?

   _____

   _____

   _____

   _____

2. How do you like to spend your time — alone or with others? What are your favorite hobbies or pastimes?

   _____

   _____

   _____

   _____

3. Which idea makes more sense to you: "An eye for an eye," or "Turn the other cheek?" Explain your answer.

   _____

   _____

   _____

   _____

4.   What are your feelings toward women? Respond to the idea that women fall into one of two categories: Madonnas or whores.

_____

_____

_____

_____

5.   Many people believe you should spend your money now because "You can't take it with you." Do you agree?

_____

_____

_____

_____

6.   Describe five ways you usually manage stress in your life.

_____

_____

_____

_____

7.   If you were in a "jam," to whom would you turn and why?

_____

_____

_____

8. Describe three things about your life that are most important to you and tell why that is true.

_____

_____

_____

9. Some experts believe that depression is really anger turned against yourself. Do you agree with that?

_____

_____

_____

10. Do you agree with the statement, "Most people are cons." Why or why not?

_____

_____

_____

11. Do you care what other people think of you? Explain.

_____

_____

_____

12. Do you agree with the statement, "Everyone is capable of murder under the right circumstances." Explain.

_____

_____

_____

13. How honest do you think you are with people who are important to you?

_____
_____
_____

14. What do you think about the comment, "It's okay for men to hug each other in affection?"

_____
_____
_____

15. Comment on the statement that "In the United States all men are penis centered."

_____
_____
_____

16. How would someone know if you were angry? What would you be doing?

_____
_____
_____

17. How do you feel about the statement that "Guilt is a useless emotion?"

_____
_____
_____

18. How would you change your life if you could?

_____

_____

_____

B. (This part of the questionnaire focuses on moral values and concepts of social deviance.)

Comment on each of the following situations, using these guidelines: (a) Is the given situation right or wrong? Harmful to anyone? Requiring legal involvement? (b) If a friend described these situations to you, implying that he or his child were involved, what advice would you give to him?

1. Two 12-year-old boys engage in mutual masturbation a couple of times.

_____

_____

_____

2. A 13-year-old boy fondles his 6-year-old sister's genitals one time.

_____

_____

_____

3. A man frequently masturbates in his car while watching attractive women on the street.

_____

_____

_____

4. In the Army, without female companionship, two het-
    erosexual men engage in frequent homosexual activi-
    ties.

    _____

    _____

    _____

    _____

5. A 10-year-old boy and his 8-year-old sister engage in
    long term fondling and mutual masturbation.

    _____

    _____

    _____

    _____

6. On a date a man coerces a woman to have sexual inter-
    course. She is unwilling and protests, but is not physi-
    cally hurt in any way.

    _____

    _____

    _____

    _____

7. A teenage boy makes obscene phone calls periodically.

    _____

    _____

    _____

    _____

8.   A man peeps in windows, masturbating as he watches females undress or have sex. He is never seen nor caught.

_____

_____

_____

_____

Appendix N
Treatment Contract

I hereby enter into an agreement with
_____ and their sex offender treatment
program to allow their staff and contracted providers to implement treatment services designed to increase nondeviant sexual behavior and arousal patterns and/or reduce deviant sexual behavior and arousal patterns. I understand that the primary goal of this treatment is to prevent me from reoffending. As part of my agreement to participate in this treatment program, I agree to the following conditions:

1. I will be completely honest and assume full responsibility for my offenses and my behavior.

2. If the treatment staff thinks it is appropriate, I agree to make a clear apology to my victim(s) and declare that what happened was not the fault of my victim(s).

3. I agree to sign a waiver of confidentiality and any other releases required either to obtain information about my behavior or to participate in therapy.

4. I will attend all treatment sessions, attend on time, and notify the appropriate staff member as soon as possible about any situation that affects my attendance or promptness. I understand that the only acceptable excuse for absence or lateness is a verifiable medical emergency.

5. I will pay my assigned fee at the time of each session unless I have made other arrangements with the staff.

6. I will not disclose any information regarding another client to anyone outside this program.

7. I will actively participate in treatment to the satisfaction of staff and other group members.

8. I understand that treatment may include individual, couples, and family therapy in addition to weekly group therapy. I also understand that treatment can be expected to last a minimum of 18 months.

9. I have been informed that treatment will include written assignments; reading assignments; counseling in such areas as stress management, assertiveness, self-esteem, sexuality, communication, and victim empathy; identifying and changing deviant behavior patterns; and developing and implementing plans to avoid high risk situations. I will be expected to discuss these tasks and assignments in group treatment.

10. I agree that my current partners, or any future significant living partners, will participate in treatment on an as-needed basis as determined by the treatment staff.

11. I agree to submit to ongoing assessment of my progress through psychological and psychophysiological evaluation as directed by the treat-ment staff.

12. I will comply with all conditions of probation and parole.

13. I will not attend any session while under the influence of alcohol or drugs.

14. I will not become verbally threatening or assaultive towards any staff member or client whether inside or outside the treatment center.

15. I understand that a staff member is on call for emergencies on a 24-hour basis.

16. I will not have any pornographic material in my possession, or use it at any time.

17. I also agree to the following special conditions

_____

_____

_____

I understand that my supervising officer will be notified immediately of any violation of this contract. I also understand that local police departments or the county sheriff's department may be contacted if necessary to maintain victim or community safety. I also understand and agree that any violation of the conditions of this contract may be grounds for termination from the program at the discretion of the treatment staff. I agree that the staff may terminate my treatment for any other problem behavior not outlined above.

I have discussed any questions I had about this contract with the person in charge of my treatment. By signing this document I give my voluntary consent to participate in all of the above under the terms stated.

_____   _____

Offender signature   Date

_____   _____

Witness signature   Date

Appendix O
Treatment Provider Application

The _____ County CSCD/District Office of the TDCJ — Pardons and Paroles Division will be referring sex offenders to treatment programs that meet certain established criteria. In order to qualify for program referrals, we ask that you submit information about your program and therapist credentials.

Please submit the following information to our office:

- Description of your organization
- Length of operation
- Kinds of clients served
- Types of treatment provided
- Treatment philosophy and approaches
- Fees
- Staff vita to include full name, social security number, kind of licensure/certification, employment history and training/education. Include specific training and experience in treating sex offenders.

Sex offender treatment providers must agree to the following requirements with all sex offenders referred to them by this office:

1. All clients must sign a waiver of confidentiality allowing the therapists and the staff of the supervising agency to communicate freely about the client and his therapy.

2. A copy of the client's intake evaluation and treatment contract should be sent to the office of the supervising agency. The intake evaluation should include information on therapeutic issues, therapy recommendations and treatment plan, and costs.

3. A referral list should be compiled each month and sent to the office of the supervising agency. When possible monthly staffings shall be arranged with the supervising officers in order to share information and impressions of the clients.

4. Whenever the client misses a therapy appointment, the supervising officer should be notified within 24 hours.

5. The supervising officer should be notified immediately whenever the therapist perceives instability, deterioration, negative attitude changes, suspected danger, or reoffenses in the client.

6. A termination report must be sent to the supervising agency whenever a client is expelled from or completes treatment.

7. The therapist should write a certified report or be willing to testify as an expert witness in hearings involving their clients.

Appendix P
Criteria for Sex Offender Treatment Providers

In an effort to ensure that the quality of services provided by therapists affiliated with the _____ County CSCD/Texas Department of Criminal Justice — Pardons and Paroles Division is of the highest professional caliber, the following criteria for contractual employment of mental health professionals as treatment providers for sexual aggressors have been adopted.

1. The mental health provider shall be listed in the Registry of Sex Offender Treatment Providers published by the Texas Interagency Council on Sex Offender Treatment.

2. The mental health provider shall have been awarded a masters degree, or other advanced graduate and/or medical degree in a nationally recognized mental health discipline. Among these disciplines are social work, counseling, psychology and psychiatry.

3. The degree work must have been completed at an accredited higher educational institution.

4. The provider shall be licensed or license eligible, and/or certified as a mental health professional.

5. The practitioner shall be proficient in group and behavioral therapy.

6. The practitioner shall have received training in traditional psychometric assessment techniques.

7. The provider must be willing to meet with representatives of the supervising agency to discuss case-related issues.

Appendix Q
Partner Alert Lists

These lists are designed to lessen the likelihood that a sex offender will reoffend. They serve to facilitate communication between the supervising officer and the offender's partner about offense-related behavior.

Changes in the Offender's Behavior Patterns

1. Abuse of alcohol and other drugs
2. Loss of control over other behaviors, e.g., smoking, gambling, battering, etc.
3. Sleep patterns
4. Tucking victim into bed without being asked to do so
5. Initiating or prolonging physical contact with the victim
6. Use of pornography
7. Sexual preoccupation
8. Difficulty accounting for his time — unstructured time
9. Cruising in a vehicle with no specific destination — unexplained mileage
10. Discipline — favoritism, harsh, erratic
11. Over-confidence regarding likelihood of reoffending
12. Not attending counseling or completing assigned tasks
13. Assuming the role of "sex educator"
14. Inappropriate apparel — robe only, no underwear, broken zipper
15. Leaving bedroom/bathroom door open
16. Job stress — fired, laid off, change in job description
17. Rapid religious conversion
18. Involvement in youth programs

19. Involvement in child's hygiene — bathing massaging, grooming, apparel

20. Selecting children's clothing — too small, adult, cosmetics;

21. Isolating the child

22. Interest in victim's social and sexual behavior

23. Reluctance to be with extended family

24. Not able to account for money, gifts, loans, purchase of drugs;

25. Uptight, anxious

26. Difficulty getting things done

27. Nonassertive

28. Change in parental responsibility — return to school/work triggers feelings of abandonment; unsupervised time

29. Offender regression — clothing, language, cultivation of younger friends

30. Unresolved marital conflicts — refusal to discuss problems

31. Change in sexual functioning — frequency, dysfunction, abuse infidelity

Changes in Victim's Behavior

1. Sleep disturbance

2. Depression

3. Social withdrawal

4. Suicide plans/attempts

5. Hygiene

6. Appetite — weight change

7. Avoidance of offender

8. Change in how victim refers to offender — from "dad" to first name basis

9. Stress in marital status — divorce

10. Fears and anxieties

11. Clinging to partner

12. Shuts and locks bedroom door

13. Stops bringing friends home

14. Protective of brothers and sisters

15. Rebellious in the home

16. Engages in theft, alcohol, drugs — other legal problems

17. Becomes physically and/or sexually abusive of others

18. Tries to escape — suicide attempts, alcohol and drug abuse, running away, out of marriage pregnancy, early marriage, sleeping elsewhere, home after curfew

19. Strives for premature adulthood

20. Seeks older acquaintances, sexual acting out, smoking, swearing, adult interests

21. Complains about illnesses that have no apparent basis in fact

22. Develops physical indicators — genital infection, rash, abrasion

23. Develops difficulties in school — discipline, truancy, homework, grades decline

24. Abruptly changes relationship with partner — angry, defiant, withdrawn

Appendix R
Chaperone Contract

Chaperone contracts are prepared by the offender and presented to the following and others if required: (1) the individual therapist, (2) the group therapists, (3) the group members, and (4) the designated chaperone. All persons may make recommendations for changes. The offender may be required to make the changes. When the final draft is presented to the group, the contract will be voted on for approval. Any therapist has equal "veto" over (1) the contents and/or (2) the choice of chaperone. The chaperone, individual therapist, and supervising officer get copies of the final approved contract.

On separate sheets of paper answer the following items.

1. List your actual offense(s) as described in your offense report/court order.

2. Describe briefly but completely exactly what you did to the victim(s) of your offense(s).

3. List all victims.

4. Describe briefly but completely and exactly what you did to each of the victims listed under #3.

5. List all deviant sexual outlets. Beside each outlet write specifically your personal rule(s) concerning that outlet. For example:

   Exposure — "When I drive around in my car, I follow a planned route to my destination."

6. Make a complete "What if" list. For example, your "what if" list would contain pro-active plans to exit a situation that brings you in contact with this type of person.

7. List observable behaviors that show your return to pattern or being in cycle, such as grooming, cruising, staring, gift giving, isolating and use of disinhibitors.

8.　List post-offense behaviors, such as withdrawal, moodiness, self-righteousness, criticalness, self-defensiveness, an over-willingness to be cooperative, setting yourself up to be taken care of by others.

9.　If your offense involves children, list observable indications of the child's response to grooming and victimization (e.g., clinging behavior, nightmares, change in eating, sleeping or hygiene habits).

10.　Statement of probability. I work daily to understand and to control my deviant thoughts, my deviant fantasies, my deviant impulses and my potential to commit sexually deviant behavior(s). I am capable of reoffense. Overconfidence is an offender trait. You should at all times be aware of my wish to present myself as "cured," determined to "never to do it again," and/or superoptimistic. (Copy this statement exactly as it appears here).

11.　The ways in which I will attempt to manipulate you include (1) attempting to weaken your surveillance of me (list ways you tend to manipulate) and (2) attempting to persuade you not to report me (list ways you tend to manipulate).

12.　Statement of Liability. If you suspect that I have reoffended or am about to reoffend, take the following action immediately:

Call my therapist(s)(list all names and phone numbers)

Call my supervising officer(list name and phone number)

Call Children's Protective Services

(if minors are involved) (list local number)

Do *not* allow me to talk you out of this action. Call within 24 hours to avoid legal consequences. Your failure to call may result in a lawsuit involving you.

13.　Statement of agreement. I hereby authorize my therapist(s), my chaperone and supervising agency staff to exchange information about me by telephone, in writing, or in person. As a chaperone you may be asked to meet with my therapist as it relates directly to your role as a chaperone. The signatures designate to all that both of you have read this contract, that you understand your responsibility, that you will report any and all suspicions of behavior(s) that may result in harm to others or in harm to the community. Your signatures also show that both of you plan to cooperate with the treatment program, with law enforcement, and ultimately the criminal justice system.

I further understand my responsibility to respect the confidentiality and the privacy of the people involved in this contract and any future persons who may become involved.

_____

Offender's printed name   Phone number

_____

Offender's signature   Date

_____

Chaperone's printed name   Phone number

_____

Chaperone's signature   Date

_____

Therapist's signature   Date

Appendix S
Conditions of Probation

1. The offender will have no direct or indirect contact with the victim(s) (or any other minors*) without the prior written consent of his supervising officer.

2. The offender will not enter onto the premises where the victim resides without the prior written permission of the supervising officer.

3. The offender will not be at any residence where minor children are residing without the prior written permission of the supervising officer. Nor will he frequent, remain about or enter into any place where minor children under the age of seventeen normally congregate.*

4. The offender will not possess any printed, photographed or recorded materials that he may use for the purpose of his deviant sexual arousal. Nor shall the offender frequent any place where such material is available to him for the purpose of deviant sexual arousal.

5. The offender will undergo a complete psychological evaluation designed to address the issue of his sexually deviant behavior. The offender will report for a sex offender evaluation to a licensed therapist approved by the Court and the supervising agency in charge of the case, on the date designated by the supervising officer in charge of the case.

6. The offender will submit to any program of psychophysiological assessment at his own expense at the discretion of the supervising officer, to include the use of the plethysmograph to assist in treatment, planning, and case monitoring. Any refusal to submit to such assessment as scheduled is a violation of the conditions of supervision.

7. The offender will submit to polygraph testing at his own expense. The testing may be recommended by the supervising

officer to determine if the defendant is in compliance with the conditions of his supervision and/or facilitate mental health treatment. Refusal to submit to such assessment as scheduled is a violation of the conditions of supervision.

8. The offender will attend and participate in the sex offender program(s) approved by the Court and the supervising officer in charge of the case. He will abide by all rules and conditions of the program and will not leave or withdraw from the program without the permission of the Court, the supervising officer in charge of the case, and the program director or his official designate, and be responsible for any costs of the program.

9. The offender will refrain from purchase, possession, or consumption of alcoholic beverages and regulated drugs.

10. The offender will submit to alcohol sensor and/or urinanalysis testing as requested by the supervising officer.

11. The offender, if found to be abusing alcohol or drugs, will participate in chemical abuse treatment approved by the Court and the supervising officer in charge of the case. He will participate in all programs offered, abide by all rules of the program, and not leave or withdraw from the program without the permission of the Court, the supervising officer in charge of the case, and the director of the treatment program or his official designate, and be responsible for any costs of the program.

12. The offender will accept no employment or participate in any volunteer activity requiring unsupervised contact with minor children under the age of 17.*

13. The offender will avoid operating a motor vehicle after dark (or during hours specified by the supervising officer when children are going to and leaving school),* except for purposes of verified employment, unless in the company of another adult deemed responsible by the supervising officer.

14. The offender will refrain from hitchhiking or picking up hitchhikers.

15. The offender will adhere to a curfew specified by the supervising officer.

16. The offender will be responsible for the costs of therapy, treatment or medical expenses incurred by the victim(s) of this or any other offense committed by the offender.

17. The offender's person, residence, or any vehicle which he may be operating, or in which he is a passenger, are subject to search at any time by his supervising officer without prior notice or search warrant to determine if he is in compliance with the conditions of his supervision. Any refusal to submit to such search is a violation of the conditions of supervision.

18. Other conditions of probation as are appropriate.

* Applicable to persons convicted of molesting children.

Appendix T
Contact With Minors

A minor is defined as anyone under 18 years of age.

Contact can mean (1) **actual physical touching**, (2) **association or relationship** (e.g., taking any action which furthers a relationship with a minor, such as writing letters, sending messages, buying presents, etc.), (3) **communication** in any form (e.g., talking, letters, etc.), and (4) **proximity** (e.g., in the same house, yard, store or restaurant where communication could be established with a minor.

If a minor is known to the offender, the offender should control the situation by leaving. It is not the minor's responsibility to avoid communication. If a minor is in a non-public place and if the minor is not going to leave, the offender should leave (e.g., a minor selling candy door to door, minors coming into your yard to play or to ask questions, minors coming to visit a friend while you are at a friend's house). This constitutes a high risk for grooming behaviors, or an opportunity (or the perception of one) for inappropriate contact.

If the minor is unknown to the offender and is in a public place (e.g., encountered in a department store, church, movie, or mall), all efforts should be made to minimize such contact by timing visits to public places when minors are not likely to be present (e.g., avoid Saturday afternoon matinees at the movies). If in spite of these efforts a minor is still encountered, the offender should not initiate any communication (verbal or nonverbal) with the minor. If a minor initiates communication, the offender should immediately move away from the minor's area. If the minor persists in trying to communicate, the offender should leave the public place.

Direct contact with a minor includes in-person visits, touching, talking on the phone, letters or written notes, and making proximity contact with a minor.

Indirect contact is making contact with a minor through another person, which includes asking the mother, teacher, or a friend to tell a minor something, or to have a minor answer questions, send pictures, deliver or receive packages, gifts, or money.

When in doubt, terminate contact immediately.

Appendix U
Glossary

abstinence violation effect. Changes in beliefs and behaviors that can result from engaging in a lapse.

adaptive coping response. A change in thoughts, feelings, or behaviors that effectively deals with a risk factor or lapse and reduces the likelihood of relapse.

anaphrodisiac. A drug or medicine that allays sexual desire.

androgen. A steroid hormone producing masculine sex characteristics and having an influence on body and bone growth and on the sex drive.

anomaly. An irregularity or defect.

antiandrogen. A substance that blocks the production of male hormones.

aphrodisiac. Anything, such as a drug or a perfume, that stimulates sexual desire.

autoerotic. Pertaining to self-stimulation or erotic behavior directed toward one's self; frequently equated with masturbation.

aversive conditioning. A behavioral technique designed to reduced deviant sexual arousal by exposing the client to a stimulus that arouses him and then introducing an unpleasant smell or touch.

bestiality. A sexual deviation in which a person engages in sexual relations with an animal. *Cf.* ZOOPHILIA.

bisexual. Literally, having sex organs of both sexes, as in hermaphrodites; having a sexual interest in both sexes.

boredom tapes. A behavioral technique wherein the client masturbates alone while talking into a tape recorder about the sexual fantasies he is using to achieve arousal.

castration. Removal of the gonads (sex glands) — the testicles in men, the ovaries in women.

circumcision. Surgical removal of the foreskin or prepuce of the male penis.

cognition. Refers to mental processes such as thinking, visualizing, and memory functions.

cognitive distortion. A thinking error or rationalization that is used to justify abusive emotions and behaviors.

cognitive restructuring. A treatment technique wherein the client is made aware of distorted thinking styles and attitudes that support sexual offending and is encouraged to change those cognitions through confrontation and rebuttal.

coitus. Sexual intercourse between male and female, in which the penis is inserted into the vagina.

collude. Cooperating with a person in such a way that they are able to continue in disapproved behavior.

congenital. Existing at birth, but not necessarily inherited.

coprophilia. A sexual deviation in which sexual gratification is associated with the act of defecation; a morbid interest in feces.

copulation. Sexual intercourse; coitus.

covert sensitization. A behavioral technique in which the deviant fantasy is paired with an unpleasant one.

cruising. The active seeking out of a victim for purposes of engaging in deviant sexual activity.

cunnilingus. The act of using the tongue or mouth in erotic play with the external female genitalia (vulva).

disinhibition. Decreasing or eliminating one's reservations or prohibitions about participating in an activity.

dyspareunia. Coitus that is difficult or painful, especially for a woman.

ejaculation. The expulsion of male semen, usually at the climax (orgasm) of the sexual act.

emission. Discharge of semen from the penis, especially when involuntary, as during sleep (nocturnal emission).

empathy. A capacity for participating in the feelings or ideas of another.

erection. The stiffening and enlargement of the penis (or clitoris), usually as a result of sexual excitement.

erotic. Pertaining to sexual love or sensation; sexually stimulating.

estrogen. A steroid hormone producing female sex characteristics and affecting the functioning of the menstrual cycle.

exhibitionism. A sexual deviation in which the individual — usually male — suffers from a compulsion to expose his genitals publicly.

fellatio. The act of taking the penis into the mouth and sucking it for erotic purposes.

fetishism. A sexual deviation in which sexual gratification is achieved by means of an object, such as an article of clothing.

frottage. A sexual deviation in which orgasm is induced by rubbing against an individual of the opposite sex, usually a stranger.

gender role. The pattern of behaviors and attitudes considered appropriate for a male or a female in a given culture.

genital organs (or **genitals** or **genitalia**). The sex or reproductive organs.

gerontosexuality. A sexual disorder in which a young person chooses an elderly person as the subject of his sexual interest.

glans clitoridis. The head of the clitoris.

gonad. A sex gland; a testicle (male) or ovary (female).

hermaphrodite. An individual possessing both male and female sex glands (ovary and testicle) or sex gland tissue of both sexes. *Cf.* PSEUDOHERMAPHRODITE.

Heterosexuality. Sexual attraction to, or sexual activity with, members of the opposite sex; the opposite of *homosexuality.*

high risk factor. An internal stimulus or external circumstance that threatens one's self-control or thus increases the risk of lapse or relapse.

homosexuality. Sexual attraction to, or sexual activity with, members of one's own sex; the opposite of *heterosexuality.*

hymen. The membranous fold that partly covers the external opening of the vagina in most virgin females; the maidenhead.

impotence. Disturbance of sexual function in the male that precludes satisfactory coitus; more specifically, inability to achieve or maintain an erection sufficient for purposes of sexual intercourse.

incest. Sexual relations between close relatives, such as father and daughter, mother and son, or brother and sister.

intellectually disabled. Mentally retarded.

intromission. The insertion of the penis into the vagina.

kleptomania. An irresistible compulsion to steal, usually without any use for the article stolen.

labia majora (sing. **labium majus**). The outer and larger pair of lips of the female external genitals (vulva).

labia minora (sing. **labium minus**). The inner and smaller pair of lips of the female vulva.

lapse. An emotion, fantasy, thought, or behavior that is part of an offender's relapse patterns.

lesbian. A female homosexual.

masochism. A sexual deviation in which an individual derives sexual gratification from having pain inflicted on him.

masturbation. Self-stimulation of the genitals through manipulation; autoeroticism.

menarche. The onset of menstruation, occurring in late puberty and ushering in the period of adolescence.

narcissism. Excessive self-love; sexual excitement through admiration of one's own body.

necrophilia. A sexual deviation in which an individual has a morbid sexual attraction to corpses.

obscene. Disgusting, repulsive, filthy, shocking — that which is abhorrent according to accepted standards of morality.

obsession. A neurosis characterized by the persistent recurrence of some irrational thought or idea, or by an attachment to or fixation on a particular individual or object.

orgasm. The peak or climax of sexual excitement in sexual activity.

orgasmic reconditioning. A behavioral technique designed to reduce inappropriate sexual arousal by having the client masturbate to deviant sexual fantasies until the moment of ejaculation, at which time the deviant sexual theme is switched to a more appropriate sexual fantasy.

ovary. The female sex gland, in which the ova are formed.

oviduct. The Fallopian or uterine tube through which the egg (ovum) descends from the ovary to the uterus.

ovulation. The release of a mature, unimpregnated ovum from one of the Graafian follicles of an ovary.

ovum (pl. ova). An egg; the female reproductive cell, corresponding to the male spermatozoon, that after fertilization develops into a new member of the same species.

paraphilia. Sexual deviations; aberrant and compulsive sexual activity often preceded and accompanied by obsessive fantasies.

pederasty. Male sexual relations with a boy; also sexual intercourse via the anus.

pedophilia. A sexual deviation in which an adult engages in or desires sexual activity with a child.

penis. The male organ of copulation and urination.

phallus. The penis, usually the erect penis.

plethysmograph. An electronic instrument that measures penile arousal (volume) while the client is presented with audio/visual materials.

pornography. The presentation of sexually arousing material in literature, art, motion pictures, or other means of communication and expression.

precocious sexuality. Awakening of sexual desire at a prematurely early age.

precursor. A general term used to encompass seemingly unimportant decisions, maladaptive coping responses, risk factors, lapses, and the abstinence violation effect; events that occur prior to a sex offense.

premature ejaculation. Ejaculation prior to, just at, or immediately after intromission; *ejaculatio praecox*.

promiscuous. Engaging in sexual intercourse with many persons; engaging in casual sexual relations.

prostate. The gland in the male that surrounds the urethra and the neck of the bladder.

prostitute. A person who engages in sexual relationships for payment.

pseudohermaphrodite. An individual who has both male and female external sex organs, usually in rudimentary form, but who has the sex glands (ovary or testicle) of only one sex, and is thus fundamentally male or female. *Cf.* HERMAPHRODITE.

puberty (or **pubescence**). The stage of life at which a child turns into a young man or young woman; *i.e.*, the reproductive organs become functionally operative and secondary sex characteristics develop.

pyromania. A compulsion, usually sexually oriented, to start fires.

rape. Forcible sexual intercourse with a person who does not give consent or who offers resistance.

rebound. A return to a deviant sexual interest following satiation.

relapse. A sexual abusive behavior or sex offense.

relapse prevention. A process for enhancing emotional, cognitive, and behavioral self-management and external supervision of sex offenders.

sadism. The achievement of sexual gratification by inflicting physical or psychological pain upon the sexual partner.

saliromania. A sexual deviation, found primarily in men, that is characterized by the desire to damage or soil the body or clothes of a woman or a representation of a woman.

satyriasis. Excessive sexual desire in a man.

scoptophilia (or **scotophilia**). A sexual deviation in which a person achieves sexual gratification by observing sexual acts or the genitals of others. *Cf.* VOYEURISM.

scrotum. The pouch suspended from the groin that contains the male testicles and their accessory organs.

seemingly unimportant decision. A decision that seems to have little bearing on whether a lapse or relapse will occur, but which actually allows the person to get closer to or further away from high risk factors that increase the probability of another offense.

semen. The secretion of the male reproductive organs that is ejaculated from the penis at orgasm and contains, in the fertile male, sperm cells.

seminal vesicles. Two pouches in the male, one on each side of the prostate, behind the bladder, that are attached to and open into the sperm ducts.

sexual intercourse. Coitus; the union of the male and female genitals.

sodomy. A form of paraphilia, variously defined by law to include sexual intercourse with animals and mouth-genital or anal contact between humans.

sperm (or **spermatozoon**). The mature reproductive cell (or cells) capable of fertilizing the female egg and causing impregnation.

testicle. The testis; the male sex gland or gonad, which produces spermatozoa.

testosterone. The male testicular hormone that induces and maintains the male secondary sex characteristics.

transsexualism. A compulsion or obsession to become a member of the opposite sex through surgical changes.

transvestism. A sexual deviation characterized by a compulsive desire to wear the garments of the opposite sex; cross dressing.

troilism (or **triolism**). A sexual deviation in which, ordinarily, three people (two men and a woman or two women and a man) participate in a series of sexual practices.

tumescence. The process of swelling or the condition of being swollen.

uterus. The hollow, pear-shaped organ in females within which the fetus develops; the womb.

vagina. The canal in the female, extending from the vulva to the cervix, that receives the penis during coitus and through which an infant passes at birth.

victim-stancing. A tendency for clients to consider themselves the real victim, no matter how aggressive their behavior towards other people.

voyeurism. A sexual deviation in which a person achieves sexual gratification by observing others in the nude. *Cf.* SCOPTO-PHILIA.

vulva. The external organs of the female, including the mons veneris, the labia majora, the labia minora, the clitoris, and the vestibule.

zoophilia. A sexual deviation that involves an abnormal degree of affection for animals. *Cf.* BESTIALITY.